H.NORMAN WRIGHT

Lessons for Life from a Bass Fisherman

The Perfect Catch

Illustrated by Sheryl Macauley

Published by Bethany House Publishers
A Ministry of Bethany Fellowship International
11400 Hampshire Avenue South
Minneapolis, Minnesota 55438
www.bethanyhouse.com

Printed in the United States of America

Library of Congress Cataloging-in-Publication Data

Wright, H. Norman.
  The perfect catch : lessons for life from a bass fisherman / by H. Norman Wright.
    p. cm.
  ISBN 0-7642-2295-3
  1. Fishing—Religious aspects—Christianity. 2. Fishers—Religious life. I. Title.
  BV4596.F5 W75 2000
242'.68—dc21   99–050953

H. NORMAN WRIGHT is an avid bass fisherman and the author of more than sixty books. He is a licensed Marriage, Family, and Child therapist and is the founder and director of Christian Marriage Enrichment. Norm's best fishing outing so far was catching and releasing thirty-eight largemouth in a single morning. He and his wife, Joyce, make their home in Long Beach, California.

SHERYL MACAULEY is an award-winning artist who specializes in creating miniature paintings on fingernails. With Norm Wright as her father, it's no surprise that she was introduced to fishing at the early age of four. Indeed, her first drawing ever was of a fish. Sheryl's largest catch to date is a 22-pound northern pike. She and her husband, Bill, live in Bakersfield, California.

To Mom and Dad who started me fishing at the age of four.

To those who have been my companions in fishing adventures:
Don, Gary, Dale, Tim, Marv, Craig, and Bill.

To my wife, Joyce, and our daughter Sheryl.

To those who have taught me how to pursue bass—the guides on the lakes across the country, and to all the pros whose articles, videos, and TV programs have made a difference in my life.

Contents

Storms of a Lifetime

1

$\mathcal{J}$ first encountered bass fishing in the early 1970s on a small lake in Montana. I went there to fish for trout and kokanee salmon but discovered a population of largemouth bass. It was a beautiful lake with lily pads at one end. Fortunately, I had a hula popper and a Jitterbug with me—and much to my surprise, they worked! It wasn't long before I noticed clouds coming across the mountain and then the lake. Flashes of lightning split the sky as the thunder grew louder. I realized that to get to my cabin I would have to go into the storm. I didn't like that idea, especially being in an aluminum boat and holding a virtual lightning rod, so reluctantly I quit fishing and headed for the nearest shore to ride out the storm (away from trees!).

A number of years ago I went fishing on a lake in Minnesota with several relatives. It was a beautiful day. As the afternoon wore on the water became very calm and the air still. Suddenly my cousin said, "Let's head for shore ... quick!" I couldn't believe my ears. The weather was great and the fish were beginning to bite. My cousin insisted, though, and by the time we made shoreline, ten minutes later, we were fighting thirty- to forty-mile-an-hour winds. For hours we huddled in our tents just waiting for them to be torn from their pegs.

Where did the storm come from? I wondered. One moment the sky had been clear, the next we were being buffeted about by strong winds and torrential rain.

Storms are like that. They often appear out of nowhere and at the wrong time, disrupting our plans. Some storms cause so much destruction that life is never the same. Other storms come with warning. They appear gradually, and weather forecasters are able to give us some indication in advance. To some degree we can prepare for these if the predictions are consistent and accurate. But often they aren't, and once again we find ourselves unprepared.

Storms come in all kinds, sizes, shapes, and intensities. There are rainstorms, hailstorms, snowstorms, windstorms, even fire storms. Nahum the prophet said, "[The Lord's] way is in the whirlwind and the storm" (1:3). I've been in some storms where the sky was split open by flashing, brilliant fingers of lightning followed by ear-deafening thunder. Once I stood on the shoreline of Jackson Lake in Grand Teton National Park and heard the thunder begin to roll through the Teton range twenty miles to the left of me and continue in front of me up into Yellowstone National Park. It was a breathtaking, awesome experience.

Not long ago my fishing partner and I were out with a guide on Castaic Lake in Southern California. It was drizzling, and now and then we heard thunder in the distance. "After my last experience, if that thunder gets any closer, we're out of here," the guide said. He told us he had been guiding a couple when a rainstorm hit. He and the other man cast their lines out, but both lines stayed well up in the air. He thought it was strange and looked back at the four rods strapped in place on the floorboard. Electricity was arcing between them! Then he noticed the woman's long red hair sticking straight out. They were in a highly charged magnetic field and a prime target for a lightning strike. They left immediately.

Moments after hearing the guide's story, I cast out. The line hung in the air. We looked at each other. Then my partner tried his hand

and his line floated, too. I don't know who was the first to say "Oh, oh," but we left as soon as we could.

That's the way it is with storms—whether in the sky or in our personal lives. They're unpredictable and often unavoidable. But what do you do when they hit? You remember. You remember the faithfulness of God. You remember that God is with you, like He was with Joshua: "No one will be able to stand up against you all the days of your life. As I was with Moses, *so I will be with you*; I will never leave you nor forsake you" (Joshua 1:5).

God was with Joseph, too: "Joseph's master took him and put him in prison, the place where the king's prisoners were confined. But while Joseph was there in prison, *the Lord was with him*; he showed him kindness and granted him favor in the eyes of the prison warden. So the warden put Joseph in charge of all those held in the prison, and he was made responsible for all that was done there. The warden paid no attention to anything under Joseph's care, because *the Lord was with Joseph* and gave him success in whatever he did" (Genesis 39:20–23). And He was with David: "In everything he did he had great success, because *the Lord was with him*" (1 Samuel 18:14).

Storms in your life do not mean God has abandoned you. He is with you. When you face adversity remember that those who survive live by faith. Scripture says, "We live by *faith*, not by sight" (2 Corinthians 5:7), and it's our own faith.

What else do you do? Remember what Jesus is able to do. In Mark 4 the disciples and Jesus were in a fierce storm that threatened to swamp their boat. The disciples were terrified, but Jesus "got up, rebuked the wind and said to the waves, 'Quiet! Be still!' Then the wind died down and it was completely calm" (Mark 4:39). Jesus can bring calm to our lives, as well.

May God who gives patience, steadiness, and encouragement help you live in complete harmony with each other—each with the attitude of Christ toward the other.

—Romans 15:5 TLB

Mr. Adaptable

$\mathcal{W}$hat do you know about bass? Well, more U.S. anglers fish for bass than for any other species. In terms of days fishing, bass take the top spot. Forty percent of all freshwater anglers fish for bass, and one out of five bass fishermen enter tournaments.

About $3 billion is spent on bass fishing each year. More guides base their livelihood on bass than any other fish. Many manufacturing companies exist because of bass fishing. This is the fish that will hit the widest variety of baits. And there are many ways to catch them, starting with your brain. It takes thought to figure bass out—but there is always a way to catch them.

The big shocker for most people is the fact that the fish you and I call a bass, well, it's not really a bass. It's actually the world's largest sunfish. There are thirty-three species that live in warm to cool water, though some fish carrying the bass name aren't related. For example, the sea bass, peacock bass, and striped bass are called bass simply because of the similar body form.

The largemouth bass has been called "Mr. Adaptable." They've adapted to many types of water. They can live in rivers or still waters. They live in man-made reservoirs and natural lakes. They live in huge lakes, and ponds of just a few acres. They can live in mining pits with stone walls, in reclaimed water, fresh water, or brackish coastal estuaries. Even though they need good quality water, they're still resilient. They can even live in salt concentrations one-third the strength of seawater. And they can live in tropical climates with alligators or in lakes that are frozen for several months.[1]

That's what I call a fish that can really flex. I wonder if we can learn something from Mr. Adaptable.

People who get along best with others have this same characteristic of adaptability. They aren't rigid and set in their ways. An adaptable person can get along with the quiet, more reserved individual as well as the nonstop talker. He or she can adjust to the organized, structured, precise, goal-oriented person as well as the hang-loose, last-minute, indecisive, spontaneous individual.

Being adaptable doesn't mean changing colors like a chameleon. It's adjusting or meshing rather than clashing. Hopefully you've learned to do this in your family. If you're an early-morning person who wakes up bright-eyed and bushy-tailed and ready to meet the day but are married to someone who opens one eye at a time with a thirty-minute interval in between, you've learned how to back off and mellow out until your spouse comes alive. If you hadn't, you wouldn't be around to read this! The book of Proverbs has an interesting insight into this particular situation: "If you shout a pleasant greeting to a friend too early in the morning, he will count it as a curse!" (27: 14 TLB).

Being adaptable means being sensitive to the uniqueness of others, then adapting how you respond to them. If you have a family member who is more of a private person, one whose energy is drained by being around people too long, hopefully you've learned that he or she is an introvert. This is the way God has wired them—it's good! If you're just the opposite, hopefully you've learned to pose questions like, "Here's something I'd like to know. Give it a few minutes and tell me what you think." Introverts will love you for it. They want to think about their answers in the privacy of their minds before giving

a response. Extroverts, on the other hand, are creatures who thrive on being around people. (They outnumber introverts three to one.) They brainstorm out loud for the whole world to hear. So, if you know an extrovert who constantly talks about buying a new 24-foot bass boat and living on it, just ask, "Are you daydreaming out loud again?" They'll probably say yes. Extroverts also need an abundance of compliments and affirmation. It's just the way God wired them.

Be adaptable in your communication style as well and you'll get along better at home and at work. Some people are expanders, revealing every detail in a conversation. Some are condensers. They give you the bottom line. Expanders like talking with expanders—condensers like talking to condensers. We're more comfortable talking to others who match our language style. So if you're married to the opposite, try talking their style for a while. Hopefully, they'll do the same for you. I know this works. I've learned to do this over the last forty years of marriage.

One last example of being adaptable and flexible: I heard about a businessman who learned to pace his conversations to those of his prospective customers. If the caller spoke slowly, he spoke slowly. If the caller spoke softly, so did he. If the caller spoke rapidly, he did the same. He credited a 30-percent increase in business to his flexibility in pacing his speech. Consider this for yourself, for Scripture calls us to be flexible and adaptable.

> Living as becomes you—with complete lowliness of mind (humility) and meekness (unselfishness, gentleness, mildness), with patience, bearing with one another and making allowances because you love one another. (Ephesians 4:2 AMP)

It only takes one time of letting your guard down and the worst can happen, just like it takes only one sloppy cast to get those hooks caught in a tree limb. What do others remember? All the times you kept your guard up or the one time you let it down? You know the answer.

Be Careful Out There

For a number of years the action-packed police television show *Hill Street Blues* captivated viewers. The offices at this precinct were occupied by a motley group of characters. In fact, you weren't sure as a viewer if you'd even want their help!

Each day a morning briefing took place. It was often chaotic and disruptive. But just before dismissing the rowdy officers, the sergeant would pause and say, "Let's be careful out there!" He was warning them to be on the alert, to keep their guard up and to never slack off because the unpredictable could and would happen.

The same advice is given to boxers. Trainers tell their fighters, "Keep your guard up. If you don't, you'll get knocked out!" Basketball coaches yell at their players to keep their hands up and keep moving to protect their basket. Fishing also requires diligence.

Jimmy Houston tells the humorous story of one of his fishing buddies out on a lake in Texas. He was fishing at night and using a topwater Jitterbug, which makes a lot of noise slurping along. About the fourth or fifth cast into the hole he was working, a big bass came up and slapped the bait with her tail. He stopped cranking and let the bait set there a long time. He gave it a twitch and she promptly jumped on it and engulfed it. He reared back and set the hook, but the line went limp. He reeled in and shot it out there again. He could see the Jitterbug wiggling across the surface. After a few more casts, he was slammed again. Once again the line went limp. Four more times the same story repeated itself. Finally the angler gave up, went to shore, tossed the rods in his truck, and headed for home.

The next night he decided to go back. When he checked his gear he discovered why he had missed those fish. The first bass had ripped the hooks right off the Jitterbug. No wonder he couldn't catch them.[2]

You always have to be careful with hooks. You have to be sure you don't snag someone else—or your clothing or the side of the boat. You have to check the hooks from time to time to make sure they're sharp, and, oh yeah, you have to make sure you still have some on the line.

Being careful is good advice for us in all areas of life. If you're a Christian you're faced with a number of issues in this world that are just begging you to lower your values and standards. There can be a tendency to slack off when you're out there with a bunch of non-Christians.

Scripture warns again and again to "be on your guard." Be on your guard, Jesus said, against hypocrisy (see Matthew 16:6–12); against greed (see Luke 12:15); against persecution from others (see Matthew 10:17); against false teaching (see Mark 13:22–23); and above all, against spiritual slackness and unreadiness for the Lord's return (see Mark 13:32–37). "Be careful," Jesus said in Luke 21:34, "or your hearts will be weighed down with dissipation, drunkenness and the anxieties of life." Being careful means to be wary, to keep your eyes open, to be alert. Let your guard down just once, and you may do something that will cause great harm.

That is why the same caution is repeated throughout the Scriptures. Listen to these warnings: "Only be careful, and watch yourselves" (Deuteronomy 4:9); "Be careful to do what the Lord your God has commanded you" (Deuteronomy 5:32); "Be careful to obey all that is written in the Book" (Joshua 23:6); "Give careful thought to your ways" (Haggai 1:5–7); "Be careful to do what is right" (Romans 12:17); "Be careful that you don't fall" (1 Corinthians 10:12); "Be careful, then, how you live" (Ephesians 5:15); and "Be careful that none of you be found to have fallen short" (Hebrews 4:1).

Where is it that you need to be careful? Who are the people you need to be most careful around? Remember, there's a reason for all the warnings. Remember these Scriptures. And it also helps to make sure you're fishing with hooks.[3]

If you are wise, your wisdom will reward you; if you are a mocker, you alone will suffer.

—Proverbs 9:12

Fishing Advisory

4

Everyone wants to give advice, whether you want it or not. Thinking we know it all, it's easy to tune out advice. Yet, we all need it from time to time. The other day I read this in the book of Proverbs: "Give instruction to a wise man, and he will be yet wiser" (Proverbs 9:9 AMP). That sounds pretty good. Most of us want to be wiser. In fact, most of us *need* a bit more wisdom. And one such area may be in how to catch more bass.

Fishing magazines like *Bass West*, *Bass Master*, and *Bassin'* are filled with opinions and advice. Recently I found this sampling:

- "Smaller and slower is better than bigger when it comes to Buzzbaits."
- "Buzzbaits are not a good choice for water below 55 degrees."
- "In fishing Spider jigs cast it beyond the target, let it sink to the bottom. Keep the rod tip at 10 o'clock while the jig is following

since bass often inhale it on the way down."

- "With crankbaits there are three general rules. The more slowly you retrieve, the deeper it will go. The lighter the line, the deeper it goes and the heavier the line the shallower it continues to run."
- "Point the rod tip at your crankbait when retrieving it and your arms will be stressed less."
- "Boat control and placement is as important to bass fishing as sharpening your hook."
- "Use lure dyes to make instantaneous color changes on the water instead of taking so many with you."
- "Make your own twin tail grubs using a soldering iron to melt the two together."

Whew. Can you remember all that? Then apply it so it sticks? And this listing just scratches the surface of all the information in a typical fishing magazine.

Some anglers devour every word and make use of what they've read. They check their mailboxes every day for the next info-packed issue. There *is* good advice in these magazines—our angling wisdom will grow. But there's another question to consider: Do we look forward to discovering wisdom from the Scripture and applying it as seriously as the next issue of a fishing publication? Magazines may help me catch more fish. God's Word can increase my wisdom of how to live my life and get along better with other anglers. Consider this passage:

> So, chosen by God for this new life of love, dress in the wardrobe God picked out for you: compassion, kindness, humility, quiet strength, discipline. Be even-tempered, content with second place, quick to forgive an offense. Forgive as quickly and completely as the Master forgave you. And regardless of what else

you put on, wear love. It's your basic, all-purpose garment. Never be without it. (Colossians 3:12–14 The Message)

This is more than advice. It's God's Word. His instruction book.

When you're out on a lake fishing for fun or in a tournament, how do you express compassion, kindness, and humility toward others?

What if someone else is hauling in the fish and you can't get a bite? What if someone races past you in a high-tech bass boat and takes that prime spot you scoped out the day before? What if you're competing with your friend in your boat for the most and biggest bass, or perhaps you're in an amateur or pro competition? How do you handle and apply what God directed Paul to say in this verse— to be "content with second place"? That could be a big order. So, how will this be reflected in your life on the lake?

Finally, brothers, whatever is true,
whatever is noble, whatever is right,
whatever is pure, whatever is lovely,
whatever is admirable, if anything is
excellent or praiseworthy—think
about such things.

—Philippians 4:8

What Are You Carrying?

5

Go around a lake and you're bound to meet a variety of people fishing. Most are friendly. They'll talk about the day, the weather, and of course, fishing. The real talkative ones not only tell you what they caught, but the size, at what depth, and what they were using. They enjoy everything around them. They joke around and have a helpful, positive outlook—even if they haven't caught a thing yet. Others walk on the dock in such an intense, focused manner they remind me of a bird dog on point. They're oblivious to life around them.

Then there's the other type of angler. You ask how it's going but immediately wish you hadn't. "Fishing is lousy. You can't believe all the stuff I've tried that doesn't work. I've used spider jigs; road runners; black and salt and pepper lizards; Rapala Fat raps; 4-inch, 6-inch, and 10-inch worms. And after all that I've only caught a couple of 2-pounders."

It makes me want to say, "If you caught two bass, you must have done something right."

It's funny how some people focus on what doesn't work or what's bad or defective instead of what's possible or what's working. It reminds me of the baseball player who was in a slump. He started watching videos of himself batting but continued to go hitless for several days . . . for good reason, it turns out. He was watching footage taken during his slump! Nothing changed until he started watching tapes from when he had hit well.

I've learned that when I'm not catching bass so well, I need to remember when I was successful. If nothing else, it helps to regain confidence. This helps in any area of our lives.

There is an old legend about three men and their sacks. Each man had two sacks, one tied in front of his neck and the other tied on his back. When the first man was asked what was in his sacks, he said, "Well, in the sack on my back are all the good things friends and family have done. That way they're hidden from view. In the front sack are all the bad things that have happened to me. Every now and then I stop, open the front sack, take the things out, examine them, and think about them." Because he stopped so much to concentrate on all the bad stuff, he really didn't make much progress in life.

The second man was asked about his sacks. He replied, "In the front sack are all the good things I've done. I like to see them, so quite often I take them out to show them off to people. The sack in the back? I keep all my mistakes in there and carry them all the time. Sure they're heavy. They slow me down, but you know, for some reason I can't put them down."

When the third man was asked about his sacks, he answered, "The sack in front is great. There I keep all the positive thoughts I have about people, all the blessings I've experienced, and all the great things other people have done for me. The weight isn't a problem. The sack is like sails of a ship. It keeps me going forward.

"The sack on my back is empty. There's nothing in it. I cut a big hole in its bottom. In there I put all the bad things that I think about myself or hear about others. They go in one end and out the other, so I'm not carrying around any extra weight at all."

What are you carrying in your sacks?

Who are you carrying in your sacks?

Which sack is full? The one full of blessings or the one on your back?[4]

> Rejoice in the Lord always. I will say it again: Rejoice!
> (Philippians 4:4)

*I press on toward the goal to win
the prize for which God has called
me heavenward in Christ Jesus.*

—Philippians 3:14

The Best Is Yet to Come

6

$\mathcal{W}$hat's the ultimate bass fishing experience for you? Ever thought about it? If you haven't, go ahead and dream a bit. What would be your peak experience?

I've heard a number of opinions. Here are a few:

- "To be able to go to one of those lakes in Mexico I always hear about and catch one hundred fish a day."
- "All I want is one week straight of nothing but bass fishing in a place like Lake Fork in Texas or Arkansas' Beaver Lake."
- "The best for me would be size—yeah, that's it. I've caught some 10-pounders, but I'd like one, say, about 15 to 17 pounds. That'd be the ultimate for me."
- "The best? No question—it will be when I step foot on my own Ranger boat—a 20- or 21-footer with everything on it."
- "To me it's making it onto the pro-tournament circle. I don't even

have to win big ones. Just to be on there and to come in near the top would be it!"

- "The best is getting to the Classic—and then winning it! I mean, what else is there?"
- "I want to get to the *Bassin'* Big Bass World Championship. If I make it there, I've arrived."

Any of these certainly would be a great experience—at least you hope they'd be. Sometimes you accomplish your dream and discover it's not what you expected. The "best" really wasn't the best.

My pastor shared a story that put a whole new slant on ultimate experiences. It seems an older lady who knew she would be dying soon went to see her minister. She wanted to talk to him about her funeral arrangements. Now, this minister had heard some strange requests during his years of ministry, but hers topped the list. She said, "Pastor, when they lay me out in that coffin I want a fork placed in my hand." He said, "A fork? What do you mean, a fork? Why that?" She replied, "Well, when we were children, we always had dessert, usually Jell-O or pudding or a cookie. But sometimes as Mama was clearing the table, she'd say, 'Children, keep your forks.' That meant dessert would be something special—like a rich, moist piece of chocolate cake or a piece of fresh-baked pie. When Mama said, 'Keep your forks', we knew the *best was yet to come*. I've had a pretty good life here on earth. But it's nothing compared to what's ahead of me when I die and see Jesus. That's the best. And it's yet to come. I want people to know. That's why I want you to put a fork in my hand."

A few months later the elderly woman died. And when people came to pay their respects, there she was, all decked out in her best clothes in a coffin with a fork in her hand. Her best had come.

What about you? Are you looking for the ultimate experience? If you know Jesus, whatever happens here on earth, your best is yet to come.

But our citizenship is in heaven. And we eagerly await a Savior from there, the Lord Jesus Christ, who, by the power that enables him to bring everything under his control, will transform our lowly bodies so that they will become like his glorious body. (Philippians 3:20–21)

O Lord, let your ear be attentive to the prayer of this your servant and to the prayer of your servants who delight in revering your name.

—Nehemiah 1:11

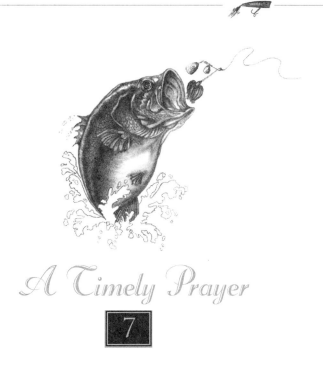

A Timely Prayer

7

Four of us were fishing from the shore. All of a sudden the rod of my partner's wife bent just about in two. I don't know who was most surprised, the three of us or her. "It's huge," she yelled. "I got a huge one." Since she hadn't fished much, advice flowed from our mouths. Fortunately, she seemed to ignore it and did all right in working that fish into shore. When it was close enough, I reached down for it, knowing I would be history if I blew it! So at the right moment I grabbed it and held it up for her to see. I wish you could have seen the expression on her face.

Later as we were talking, she said, "Oh, I've got something to admit to all of you." That sure got our interest. "When I was fighting that fish . . . I prayed. I prayed that I'd get it in." We laughed, and I replied, "Well, there's nothing wrong with that. I've done the same thing."

I don't think there are any limits as to when or what you pray for as long as it's in the will of God. In 1 John 5:14 we're told, "And this is the confidence which we have before Him, that, if we ask anything according to His will, He hears us" (NASB). I'll leave it up to you to decide if landing a fish counts. Nevertheless, prayer is our opportunity to talk with the One who loves us most.

I like what Patrick Morley said about prayer in *The Seven Seasons of a Man's Life*:

> One day I was trying to decide if I should send a copy of a letter I received from President Clinton to our ministry partners list. It didn't feel right. I talked it over with a man in our office but couldn't get closure. As I was concluding the conversation, I said, "Well, I'll keep praying about it." Just then it hit me that I had been thinking about it, but not actually praying. There is a huge difference between thinking and praying. I prayed, and immediately the answer came—don't send it.
>
> When a friend of mine became deathly ill with cancer, another friend asked me how he was doing. "He's a very sick boy," I said. "I guess the only thing we can do is pray."
>
> "No," he corrected. "The thing we *can* do is pray." What gave his statement added authority was that he offered this advice just six months after his own wife of twenty-six years had died from cancer.
>
> Another friend was going through a crisis at work. He said, "I've tried everything I can think of. I guess I'll pray."
>
> Why is prayer the last thing we do and not the first? Why don't we pray more? First, we pray last or don't pray at all because we don't believe prayer will really work. If we really believed God would answer our prayer we would pray all the time. If we *really* understood prayer, it would be the principal habit of our hearts. It would be our first resort, not our last.

Second, prayer is hard work. One day I was in the car with Bill and Vonette Bright. At the time Vonette was the chair of the National Day of Prayer—she even got Congress to make it a law! I nearly ran off the road when she said, "Prayer is hard work. Sometimes I find it hard to concentrate. My mind wanders." Well, I already knew that was true for me! I just couldn't believe it was true for one of the world's most famous pray-ers! What an encouragement! Misery loves company. Prayer is hard work. Sometimes it's hard to stay focused. Besides that, no one holds us accountable to pray.

God wants us to pray. Prayer is man speaking to God. Prayer is how we communicate with God. Prayer changes things. However, God doesn't answer petitions that are not presented. If we go about solving our challenges in our own strength, we rob God of the glory He wants for himself. He would rather that we come humbly before the throne of His grace so that He can give us mercy and help in our times of need.

Prayer changes us. Prayer breaks strongholds. Prayer determines the destinies of men, their families, their communities, and their nations.

So, what is your prayer life like? Is prayer a significant part of your life? Do you sense a close, personal communion with Jesus when you pray? It can happen. And He's waiting to hear from you.[5]

Listen to me, my people, my chosen ones! I alone am God. I am the First; I am the Last.

—Isaiah 48:12 TLB

A Life-Changing, Unchanging God

8

$\mathcal{I}$f you could watch a videotape of yourself fishing five years ago, what would you see? Would you be casting, jigging, or searching out bass the same ways as today? Some people would. They get into a routine and think, *Hey, it's worked for years. Why mess with it?*

But in bass fishing you've got to be able to switch gears. Bass change their habits, even shorelines change. A reservoir I fish numerous days a year is fifteen feet lower this year than last, so I've had to change my tactics. (I'm also taking many pictures so I'll remember the shoreline when the lake fills up.)

You can go to a lake determined to use your favorite lures, but if the only thing that's working is shad, you'd better use shad. One day I met a guide at Casitas Lake ready to do battle with the bass. Four hours later he sent me home (and didn't charge me a thing) because he was unable to catch any shad to use for bait. He said we'd just waste our time without them. Some dyed-in-the-wool "artificial" bass anglers went out anyway, and sure enough, they were shut out.

I know change is sometimes necessary, but I still resist it! How about you? It's okay to admit it. We get comfortable with our routines. It's not that we can't change; it's just that we'd rather not. Not all change is bad. We just don't want to move out of our comfort zone to experience it.

These days we're seeing more changes than most people can handle. Just about the time you get used to a new computer and printer, it's out-of-date. By the time you make your first few payments on a new bass boat, newer models are being introduced. Each season the new edition of Bass Pro catalog comes out. Page after page has the word *New* blazed across it. And we study it. Who knows? This could be *the* lure of all lures.

But let's think about character change for a minute. In what ways are you different today than five years ago (aside from the obvious: age!)? Hopefully changes have improved the quality of your character.

Although change is a part of life, God is known by His *changelessness*. Imagine this: You're at work, and someone walks into the office and makes the following statement:

> Let me tell you something about God that you may not know. God doesn't ever learn a thing. He knows all things. He doesn't have to go around spying on people to discover what's going on; He knows. Remember when you were in school and struggled to learn something? Well, God cannot learn and has never learned. He doesn't need to. He knows everything instantly. He knows everything equally well. He never wonders about anything, never

discovers anything, and is never amazed by anything. He also knows all the possibilities that can happen.[6]

God doesn't change. Created things have a beginning and ending, but God doesn't. He has always been and always will be. There was not a time when He did not exist. He does not grow older. He does not get wiser, stronger, or weaker. He cannot change for the better. He is perfection. Scripture confirms this.

> They shall perish, but you go on forever. They will grow old, like worn-out clothing, and you will change them like a man putting on a new shirt and throwing away the old one! (Psalm 102: 26 TLB)

God's character does not change. He *is* truth. His truth does not change. Because He *is* mercy, He never has to take back what He has said. His mercies toward us are new every morning. Because He *is* goodness, you can know that every good and perfect gift comes from Him. Because He is the promised Lamb of God, you can trust in His promises and know that He will fulfill them concerning your life. God's *purposes* do not change. What God does in the context of time, He planned from eternity. All that He has committed himself to do in His Word will be done.

James speaks about God as one "with whom there is no variation or shadow due to change" (1:17 RSV). This verse refers to the fact that when a sundial is at high noon, it does not cast a shadow. God is always at high noon for you. You can depend upon Him. What a comfort.

It's difficult to understand everything about God with our minds. But our inability to comprehend gives evidence to the vast difference between God and the people He created.[7]

So the next time you're out there alone on the water and want something to occupy your mind for a while, think about how God doesn't change. In fact, write down what James said about God and read it over while you're on the water. Discovering that we can count on God *not* changing gives us stability.

It is the Lord your God you must follow, and him you must revere. Keep his commands and obey him; serve him and hold fast to him.

—Deuteronomy 13:4

What Kind of Fish Are You?

9

Jim Grassi is the founder of Let's Go Fishing Family Ministries as well as a versatile fisherman. He's fished with some of the top bass pros and many professional athletes. In one of his books, *Heaven on Earth—True Stories of Fishing and Faith*, he tells about a 6-foot-8 former basketball player, Jay Carty. Jay wrote a book called *Something's Fishy*. In it he presented a unique correlation between certain types of fish and our Christian commitment to be followers of Jesus. Jim embellished a few of these definitions. Here are three species of fish:

Carp—(1) A trash fish. Carp are bottom-feeders. As they cruise the murky waters, their ugly lips turn downward and play vacuum cleaner, sucking up all the junk they can find. They're scavengers and scum suckers. They especially enjoy fish eggs.

Like rats, carp are prolific breeders. (2) People who feed on the debase and immoral things of the world. (3) Sin that renders a believer powerless, which subsequently keeps a nonbeliever from believing.

Bass—(1) A game fish that is weary and protective. Bass carefully guard their territory and keep a vigilant eye on every aspect of their environment. They seem to have passion, a disposition that creates excitement and zeal for life. They are alert and very selective feeders. (2) A sold-out, on-fire, goin'-for-it, Jesus-lovin' believer. A true disciple.

Trout—(1) A game fish that sometimes acts like a bass. Trout are not as protective about their nests and will readily eat their young. They sometimes hang out with other species, thereby confusing anglers looking at electronic fish locators who are trying to determine what type of fish they have under their boat. In a stream they can be found right next to trash fish like suckers, carp, or squawfish. (2) A lukewarm Christian. A person trying to live in both worlds. "Trout" are spiritually immature. Most people assume "trout" are saved, but they are either carp or bass dressed up to look like trout.

There's an age-old, seldom-told story about three ugly troutlings that is similar to the ugly duckling story. As the tale was told by Jay:

Three little trout were raised in separate ponds.

Carp ate the first ugly troutling [in the first pond].

The second ugly troutling [in the second pond] discovered he was a bass. As soon as he realized it, he ate the carp.

The third ugly troutling [in the third pond] was a carp. But the bass thought he was a trout and didn't eat him. Since the bass thought this, the carp thought he was a trout, too. So the other fish let the carp they thought was a trout live in the pond. He grew up, got married, and had lots of little carps who were raised to think they were trout.

There were then so many trout that quite a few of the bass wished they could be trout, and began dressing like them. Now there are so many carp who think they are trout and so many bass who look like trout, the bass are being squeezed out of the pond. That's what happens when you let a little carp into your pond.

One day the sky that Chicken Little thought was falling actually did fall. All the fish in the third pond were killed. Carp do not go to fish heaven, but bass do. None of the carp who thought they were trout went. And there weren't many bass left to go. . . . There is something fishy in Christendom and I know what it is: Carp.

What are you—a bass, a trout, or a carp? Truly committed disciples (bass) are those who are growing in their faith and service. They sense a call to accountability and responsibility for themselves and others. True believers realize that discipleship requires both a Christ-like attitude and resulting actions.[8]

*To him who overcomes, I will grant
to eat of the tree of life, which is in
the Paradise of God.*

—Revelation 2:7 NASB

$\mathcal{S}$urvivors

10

$\mathcal{B}$ass are tough. They're survivors. They have to be. When they're small, all sorts of predators with fins or feathers would love to devour them. As bass get larger they risk another danger—anglers. Soon they feel a hook in their jaw—some feel it again and again and again. I wonder just how many times some bass have been caught during their lifetime! They learn to survive.

I'm impressed by survivors. They've overcome obstacles to get the most out of life. There are anglers who fish with one arm, others from a wheelchair. They have a choice. They could have given up on fishing and said, "Forget it. I can't do it." But they didn't. These are guys and gals who won't let life overcome them.

Scripture talks about those who overcome. In the book of Revelation (NASB) we find statements to the churches that are being judged. Each time, words of great hope and encouragement are given to "him who overcomes." It is to the overcomers that the Lord makes these promises:

> "He who *overcomes* shall not be hurt by the second death" (2:11).
>
> "To him who *overcomes*, to him I will give some of the hidden manna, and I will give him a white stone, and a new name written on the stone which no one knows but he who receives it" (2:17).
>
> "And he who *overcomes*, and he who keeps My deeds until the end, to him I will give authority over the nations . . . and I will give him the morning star" (2:26, 28).
>
> "He who *overcomes* shall thus be clothed in white garments; and I will not erase his name from the book of life, and I will confess his name before My Father, and before His angels" (3:5).
>
> "He who *overcomes*, I will make him a pillar in the temple of My God, and he will not go out from it any more; and I will write upon him the name of My God, and the name of the city of My God, the New Jerusalem, which comes down out of heaven from My God, and My new name" (3:12).
>
> "He who *overcomes*, I will grant to him to sit down with Me on My throne, as I also overcame and sat down with My Father on His throne" (3:21).

Tom Sullivan has been a frequent guest on the *Good Morning America* program. He has also had acting roles on *M*A*S*H*, *Fame*, and *Airport '77*. Tom holds two national championship records in wrestling and was on the 1958 Olympic team for the United States. He holds a degree from Harvard in clinical psychology; he is a musician and author, he runs six miles a day on the beach, he skydives . . . and he is blind. He can't see a thing. His life was portrayed in the gripping film *If You Could See What I Hear*.

When Tom speaks to large crowds, the audience is with him all the way, listening, applauding, laughing, and learning from a man who cannot see the enjoyment on their faces. In his presentation, he has one major point: "You've got a disadvantage? Take advantage of it! People don't buy similarity. They buy differences." A disadvantage is what makes you stand out. Think about it. If you're similar to everyone else, you blend in and get lost in the crowd.

Tom shared about the time when as an eight-year-old he heard some new sounds in his backyard—the crack of a bat as it hit a ball and the thud of the ball as it struck a glove. He listened some more and de-  cided some kids were playing a game. Did he get discouraged because he was blind and couldn't see what was happening? Not at all. He found a rock and a stick and taught himself how to bat. He wasn't sure where to hit, so he devised a target to aim at. He set up a transistor radio on a tree stump, walked back a few steps, and began to practice. Eventually he could hit the radio every time.

After a while Tom told his dad that he wanted to play baseball. Most people would have said, "You want to do *what?*" Instead, Tom's dad replied, "Really? . . . Uh, which position?" Tom said, "I want to be a pitcher." Can you imagine the silence that hung in the air after that statement? His dad talked to the manager of the local Little League team and was able to get Tom on the team. And indeed, he pitched. They had another boy stand next to him to catch the ball when the catcher threw it back.

In Tom's presentation he tells the audience, "Can you picture this frightened little nine-year-old coming up to the plate, knowing that a blind kid is on the mound ready to throw a ball at him?" After he knocked out several boys, he switched to wrestling. Probably a collective sigh of relief went up from every Little League team.

Tom has a great sense of humor. He can even pop out his glass eyes, which he claims helped him win a few wrestling matches.[9]

It's an amazing story. Tom had a choice between cynical self-pity or learning to live a courageous life. Each of us has the same choice. Listen to one last statement by this man: "I've determined that my disadvantage in life is blindness. I will therefore become, as a blind person, all that I can possibly be. That will become my distinctive message."[10]

Be Still

11

The water is quiet. No sound of outboards. No planes overhead. Just the sounds of nature. The wind moving through the trees, the buzz of flies and dragonflies, the lapping of the water, the sound of a pair of western grebes dancing across the lake surface. That's what it's all about. Sure, there's the fishing, that too. But breaking away from man-made sounds to hear what we rarely hear, that's when our bodies and minds can relax.

Do you hear nature when you get on the lake? Listen to the sounds. They're there. Some anglers hear them. They listen for them. Some never hear them. They take their intense pace of daily living and put it on their pursuit of bass. That's why they're always stressed. They're hurrying through life. They take their hurrying sickness with them wherever they go.

When you hurry through life you lose touch with those around you. You can't hear what others say to you. You can't hear God's voice. He has a message for you: "Cease striving and know that I am God" (Psalm 46:10 NASB). Ken Gire talks about this:

> The call to be still, to stand silent, to cease striving, comes in the context of a life in chaos. A life surrounded by landslides, tidal waves, and earthquakes. Whether the chaos is environmen-

tal, political, relational, emotional, or simply organizational, there is a river, the psalmist tells us, that flows from the throne of God. A river that remains clear and refreshing, undisturbed by the upheavals. A river whose streams bring gladness. The gladness we can have in the midst of turbulent times, the peace that flows like a river, is the nearness of God.

"The Lord of hosts is with us," the psalmist assures us. "The God of Jacob is our stronghold" (46:11 NASB).

He is with us when our world caves in around us. When the marriage others looked up to slips into the heart of the sea. When once-calm relationships now roar and foam. When the once-stable mountain of financial security now quakes.

He is "our refuge and strength" (46:1).

"A very present help in trouble" (46:1 RSV).

We will never know it, though, unless we cease striving and still our heart. Could this prayer describe the way you feel at times?

Lord, I feel like a mouse on a treadmill.
Rushing around, faster and faster.
Getting nowhere.
And the first thing that goes out the window is you.
No time, Lord, sorry!
Then my family.
They should know I'm busy and not ask for my time!
And my friends.
Can't they see all the things I have to do?
Lord, it's at times like this that I need you most.
Yet you seem so far away.
Why, Lord? Where have you gone?
Then I hear it, the quiet voice . . .
. . . be still, and know that I am God.

You are near. You have been all the time.

And I understand that I can't hear you if I don't give time to you. Lord, I just thought so much depended on me. I know the whole world wouldn't end if I took a break, but it made me feel important. I need to remember that it's your world, your work. I'm glad to have a part in it, but it's yours, not mine. And when I've done what I can, I can safely leave the rest to you.

—Eddie Askew

A Silence and a Shouting[11]

Endure hardship as discipline; God is treating you as sons. For what son is not disciplined by his father?

—Hebrews 12:7

Stubborn or Determined?

Some anglers give up easily. They make a few casts into a prime area, and when nothing happens they move on. A few hours later they come into the dock and say, "Man, we covered the entire lake and nothing was biting. And now this lousy rain. We're just getting too wet and miserable. When I fish, I want to catch fish and want to stay dry." Inevitably, at the end of the day another boat arrives and the occupants have a totally different story. The two guys in the second boat survived several hours of rain and didn't come close to covering the entire lake, but they worked different points and areas of structure again and again. They caught and released fish most of the day. If one lure didn't work, they tried something else. They varied the speed of their retrieve and eventually tied into the fish they were after. These guys were determined and patient; they knew what would work and were willing to follow their beliefs.

Sounds like a pretty good pattern for the rest of our life, doesn't it? It takes determination, patience, and yes, even stubbornness, to survive in today's world. But it was no different in olden days. The Bible tells us about a guy who was so stubborn that even when the ruler of his country started hassling him, he wouldn't budge. He stood his ground, even when thousands of people he was supposed to lead disagreed with him. And they weren't silent in their disagreement. They griped and complained and blamed, and finally . . . rebelled. And to make it worse (maybe you've been in this pressure cooker), his own family—his brother and sister—got on his case and became his personal critics. But this guy wouldn't budge even one inch. Talk about stubborn. Or was he?

Scripture uses another word to describe Moses. He *endured*. He wouldn't cave in or throw in the towel. When someone is having a hard time we often say, "Hang in there." That's exactly what Moses did. Look at how other translations put it.

The *Living Bible* says he ". . . kept right on going."

The *New English Bible*: ". . . he was resolute."

The *Amplified Bible*: ". . . he held staunchly to his purpose."

Moffatt's rendering: ". . . he never flinched."

By faith he left Egypt, not fearing the king's anger; he persevered because he saw him who is invisible. (Hebrews 11:27)

Chuck Swindoll says we should . . .

Stand firm when conspirators seem to prosper. Stand firm when the wicked appear to be winning. Stand firm in times of crisis. Stand firm even when no one will know if you compromised. Stand firm when big people act contemptibly small. Stand firm when petty people demand authority they don't deserve. Stand firm . . . keep your head . . . stay true . . . endure.[12]

A friend loves at all times, and a brother is born for adversity.

—Proverbs 17:17

Friendly Crawdads

13

$\mathcal{K}$now much about crawdads? Sure, they look like miniature lobsters, but anything else? There are over three hundred species of crawdads (or crayfish) in the United States, and they're important to the food chain. Basically, they have two major activities in life—growing and breeding. After the eggs are laid, they hatch in two to twenty weeks (depending on the water temperature). Crawdads start off the size of pinheads but molt in order to grow. The crawdad chemically dissolves the old shell and the molting starts. For a couple of days the crawdad is defenseless. In the first year of life this molting usually occurs four to ten times. In the second year it occurs one to four times. Most crawdads don't live more than two years—in part because bass love them. Especially large bass.

I use crawdads especially with smallmouth at one particular lake. Not only are they great for fishing, they also provide a lot of laughs.

After one trip I brought some back in a container for the small pond in my backyard. (No, I don't fish there. It's *very* small, and in it I raise tropical fish.) When I arrived home, guess what had tipped over in the back of the van! Well, I thought I had found them all, so I dumped them in the pond. A couple of months later I got a start as I did a thorough cleaning under the seats of the van. Here was a specimen perfectly preserved. No smell. No mess. Imagine the difference if it had been a fish!

A couple of years later a fairly large repairman came out to check a problem with our phone lines. To get to some of the lines he had to crawl under our house. He lifted the trapdoor, saw how tight it was going to be, muttered some indecipherable words, and crawled in, keeping low to the ground because of his size and the proximity of pipes and two-by-fours. As he crawled along it was easier to keep his head down and look up every few feet to see where he was. Suddenly his gaze fastened upon two outstretched claws about six inches from his face. I wish I could have seen how big his eyes got. A crawdad had ventured out of the pond. Now, this wasn't an ordinary one. This was the Godzilla of the crawdad kingdom. He was huge, at least eight inches long, and he was deceased. I mean, dead—petrified in the claws out, defensive "kill the enemy" position. As I said, he was just inches away from the repairman. Shock barely describes his response. It freaked him out. Remember him crawling in slowly? That was low gear. Going out he tromped on the accelerator . . . backwards. Know what happens when you crawl backwards? Your butt goes up in the air. Not a good idea with pipes, two-by-fours, and nails to hit. Needless to say he came out an unhappy camper. He even questioned the heritage of the builders of our home! He called his supervisor and said, "There ain't no way I'm going back under there. You get someone else!" And with that he left.

Sure enough, another guy came, fixed the phone lines, and retrieved Godzilla crawdad. I had to admit, he *was* fierce-looking. And I think the phone company put an asterisk by our house number for future reference.

Craig, a fishing friend in Alabama, was having trouble finding crawdads, so I decided to surprise him with some at a counselors' convention in Nashville. I mean, why not? What are friends for? I bought the crawdads, put them in a flat Tupperware container, poked some holes in it, and headed for the airport. I wish you could have seen the security guard's expression as the container went through the screening machine. He couldn't figure it out, so I showed him. He looked at me, then back to the crawdads. I'm not sure he understood, but he smiled and gave me the okay. Well, one potential obstacle down, one to go—boarding the plane. It went great. The flight attendant asked what they were, so I told her. "Really?" she said. "Yeah," I replied, "I brought them for a snack. I might get hungry."

Once at the hotel, I figured the critters were probably kind of cramped, so I drew some water in the tub, plopped them in, and went to bed. The next morning I went down to the conference for all-day meetings. At some point I let my mind drift and it suddenly dawned on me . . . housekeeping! *Oh my gosh! I hope I didn't give someone a heart attack when they went into the bathroom to clean it.* The more I thought about it the more I wished I had set up a video camera to see their reaction. As I imagined the scene I began to chuckle. My Alabama friend, who didn't know about my surprise yet, turned to me and in his drawl said, "Hey, what y'all laughin' about?" I just shook my head and said, "Nothing—tell ya later."

After the evening meeting I took Craig to my room and told him that I had brought a present from California. "It's in the bathroom," I said. "The bathroom?" he asked as he ventured in. Within moments he was laughing hysterically. "I don't believe it. I just don't believe it. Y'all are crazy." My last image of Craig that night was walking down the hall of the Marriott carrying crawdads, shaking his head, and laughing uncontrollably.

That's one of the best things about friends. You can have a lot of fun and make some great memories, so don't overlook the value of a friend.

> A man of many companions may come to ruin, but there is a friend who sticks closer than a brother. (Proverbs 18:24)
> Perfume and incense bring joy to the heart, and the pleasantness of one's friend springs from his earnest counsel. (Proverbs 27:9)

Because God wanted to make the unchanging nature of his purpose very clear to the heirs of what was promised, he confirmed it with an oath. . . . We have this hope as an anchor for the soul, firm and secure.

—Hebrews 6: 17, 19

Cast Your Anchor

14

$\mathscr{A}$nchors come in all shapes and sizes. There are mushroom-shaped anchors, navy anchors, chain anchors, and even tri-fluted river anchors, which use three blades to provide a grappling action. I've also heard of an adjustable sea anchor called the Driftmaster. Of course, with so many anchors come all sorts of anchor accessories, including power winches, anchor runs, and anchor pulleys.

Anchors are essential for bass boats. But as you may know, anchoring a boat is not as simple as some people think. You don't just pull up to a spot and heave the anchor over the side to drop straight down. There's an art to doing it properly. The first time I hired a bass guide I was amazed at what he did. He found the spot he wanted to be on but motored past it. About thirty yards away, he dropped the first anchor. Then he returned to his selected spot and went out thirty yards the opposite direction to drop the second anchor. There he proceeded to pull on the first line until the two were equidistant. We were secure. No one was about to move.

Of course, things can go wrong with anchors. If you've got just one, you're likely to swing all over the place. Then there are times when your anchor gets caught on the bottom, and I mean really caught. Once I was smallmouth fishing over a group of boulders, but when it came time to pull the anchor up and move . . . nothing happened. We tried everything, but that anchor was history. It's probably still there today. When that happens, we just say the lake "ate" our anchor.

One of the most common problems is when your anchor won't hold. It just won't grab onto the bottom. The slightest breeze begins to move you. Soon you're off the fish, and you end up spending most of your time moving around and trying to get that anchor to hold. Meanwhile, you drift.

It's easy to drift around in life as well. You can spend years planning and striving, but when something goes wrong, you feel adrift. We need something in life we can depend on—that won't drift with the wind or the currents. Only one anchor does this with 100 percent certainty—the Word of God. It's certain. It won't change.

> The law of the Lord is perfect, reviving the soul. The statutes of the Lord are trustworthy, making wise the simple. The precepts of the Lord are right, giving joy to the heart. The commands of the Lord are radiant, giving light to the eyes. The fear of the Lord is pure, enduring forever. The ordinances of the Lord are sure and altogether righteous. They are more precious than gold, than much pure gold; they are sweeter than honey, than honey from the comb. By them is your servant warned; in keeping them there is great reward. (Psalm 19:7–11)

In his book *The Seven Seasons of a Man's Life*, Patrick Morley says:

Frankly, after more than twenty years of following Christ, I find I no longer read my Bible. My Bible reads me. On its crinkly pages *I see myself*—my motives, my ambitions, my longings, my pain, my sufferings, my sins, my hope, my joy. As the rustling pages turn, *I see God*—His love, His forgiveness, His birth, His death, His resurrection, His sovereignty, His holiness, His character.

I love my Bible. I love the Bible because I don't have to worry about receiving flash updates or corrective bulletins. I don't have to worry about a factory recall. I don't have to be concerned about whether or not a retraction will appear in tomorrow's version. I love my Bible because it is true, and truth doesn't change. In a world awash with change, I'm glad to have an anchor, a solid rock upon which to build my life.[13]

It's all right to take the time to bring up memories and reflect on them. Our past is part of our present life.

Abundant Memories

One morning my fishing partner went out to the reservoir where we fish dozens of times a year. I was out of town and couldn't join Don, but if there ever was a day I should have been there, this was it. Not to fish, but rather to watch.

It was a breezy day, and several miles away a raging brush fire was sweeping through the hills, spurred on by intense winds. The fire was still far enough away for him not to be alarmed, so Don headed out to a favorite spot in a corner next to the dam. He landed a couple and after a while he could hear the rotor blades of an approaching helicopter, nothing unusual since the reservoir was under the flight path of the El Toro Marine Base. But this helicopter sounded louder than normal. All of a sudden it passed over Don's head, headed for the middle of the lake, and then hovered there. Underneath, dangling from a long cable, was a huge bucket. Don realized the chopper was part of the fire-fighting service, and they were using the reservoir's water.

Don watched the water extraction, enjoying the unusual sight. He enjoyed it, that is, until the pilot got his load and took off, returning along the same flight pattern as before. You got it! As the helicopter flew over Don, water sloshed out and drenched him! And this didn't happen just once. He experienced this shower again—and again. After the third time Don headed for shore and went home soaked. To this day I wonder what that pilot must have thought. *Well, maybe this guy enjoys getting wet. Or, maybe he just takes a while to learn.*

Two days later Don and I met to fish. Walking on the dock I was shocked by how much water was in our twelve-foot aluminum boat. "Would you look at this," I said, momentarily forgetting about Don's "shower" experience. "Where did this come from?" I asked. My partner (normally a man of few words) didn't say a thing as I started to bail out the water. Then it dawned on me. "It's from that helicopter the other day, isn't it?" To which he replied simply, "Yup." We both burst out in laughter.

Fishing sure can make some great (and unusual) memories. One of the delights of life is to reflect back and remember these events. Our memory is a gift from God.

David, writing in the psalms, pointed out how memories of God's great work are passed from one generation to another:

> Great is the Lord, and highly to be praised;
> And His greatness is unsearchable.
> One generation shall praise Thy works to another,
> And shall declare Thy mighty acts.
> On the glorious splendor of Thy majesty,
> And on Thy wonderful works, I will meditate.
> And men shall speak of the power of Thy awesome acts;

And I will tell of Thy greatness.
They shall eagerly utter the memory of Thine abundant
    goodness,
And shall shout joyfully of Thy righteousness.
    (Psalm 145:3–7 NASB)

That's an interesting thought: They utter the memory of God's goodness. Sometimes I forget all that God has done for me. Do you have the same problem?

Sometimes I forget the way God has guided me. Has this ever happened to you?

Sometimes I forget the way God has intervened for me. Sound familiar?

Now and then I sit down and reflect on my spiritual journey. I remember the day I invited Jesus Christ into my life. When did that happen to you? With whom have you shared this recently?

I remember when God guided and called me into my life's work. Have you thought about your story for a while? Who knows how God has directed you?

I remember when God amazed me by opening doors for me that I never knew existed. Has this happened for you?

I remember His comfort during life's losses and hard times. Have you experienced this, as well?

And I remember His faithfulness not just in the past, but in what He will be doing in the future. I trust that you will remember this, too.

Seek first his kingdom and his righteousness, and all these things will be given to you as well.

—Matthew 6:33

Called to. . .?

Earlier I introduced you to Jim Grassi, an all-around sportsman and the founder of Let's Go Fishing Family Ministries and the Fellowship of Christian Anglers Society. Jim speaks to nearly four hundred thousand people annually.* He was an up-and-coming fishing pro on the tournament circuit when he felt another calling. Here's his story:

In the late 1970s, my success on the western black bass tournament trail grew with each event. Fishing was becoming the passion of my life. I was now being asked to host fishing television programs, do demonstrations for major sports shows, and write for several major publications. In addition, a community college asked me to teach three classes a week on fishing.

All this, on top of my accomplishments in public adminis-

*For more information about Jim Grassi and Let's Go Fishing Family Ministries, write to PO Box 3303, Post Falls, ID 83877 or call (208) 457–9619.

tration and my award-winning park and recreation programs, placed me among the top administrators on the West Coast. My MPA (Master of Public Administration degree) and other academic achievements qualified me to advance quickly in the organizations I served.

The climb to the top had not been easy. It required that I make some personal sacrifices along the way. My faith and my family had been put on the back burner so I could chase the "great American dream"—success.

I was fortunate when it came to family. God gave me a wonderful wife with enormous patience and love. Louise was the glue that kept our family together. Our gifted twin sons—Dan and Tom—required special attention and a great deal of Louise's time. The kids were a special blessing, and, of course, I took most of the credit for that, too.

After a childhood of low self-esteem and hard knocks, I found it difficult to adjust to all the good things happening in my life without being prideful. I began to think I could do no wrong. But I was just kidding myself.

This brings to mind a fishing story that perfectly illustrates the overconfidence and arrogance I displayed during that time in my life. One of the nation's top fishing pros had become so successful that he was regularly invited to give talks about his techniques. To save time and prepare for the lectures, he hired a driver at minimum wage.

The pro was earning over $1,000 per lecture and was feeling pretty good about himself. After hearing about 50 seminars, the driver commented that he could probably give the same lecture and people would never know the difference.

The pro was fascinated with the driver's comment and decided to test the theory by trading places with him at the next stop. The chauffeur got all decked out with the pro's shirt and took the podium as the real pro stood in the back of the room observing. Sure enough the chauffeur did a great job and had the audience totally convinced that he was a professional.

Just as the chauffeur completed his last thought, however, a gentleman in the back asked him an extremely technical question about using electronic fish finders. To avoid giving himself away, and to maintain his prideful appearance, the chauffeur responded to the inquiry, "You know that really is an easy question; in fact, I believe my chauffeur [the real 'pro'] standing in the back of the room can even answer that."

Like the chauffeur, I had begun to think I had all the answers to everything. I had seen enough good parents and heard a few sermons on God's plan for the home. I thought I could take all this to most onlookers.

By all *outward* appearances, I was a successful businessman, fisherman, college professor, outdoor writer, consultant, husband, and father. To top it off, I received a new Ranger consignment bass boat that was the envy of every friend I had. Life was very good to me. But was it as fulfilling as I wanted it to be?

My wife did not think so. She arranged for us to attend James Dobson's parenting conference at Mount Hermon Christian Conference Center in the Santa Cruz mountains. I had no tournaments scheduled and no excuse for not attending. My only consolation was that my good friend and fishing buddy Jerry had also been roped into this event by his wife, and we would drive to the camp together.

As we made our way to the conference center, Jerry and his wife, Jeanie, shared their plans to adopt a little girl from Chile. They asked me, "What does it take to be a good parent?" I said boastfully, "Just spend some quality time with the kids and they will do just fine."

My idea of being a successful parent was to beat the national average for quality time that dads spend each day with their children—37.5 *seconds*. I did that every night when I came home from my night meetings. I would go into the boys' room with a flashlight to see how much they had grown since my last visit. I prayed over them and tenderly kissed them goodnight.

Dr. Dobson was already preaching as we walked in on the first session. Within ten minutes, he informed us he would no longer be doing conference programs because it was taking too much time away from his family. He then explained that kids need both quality *and* quantity time from *both parents* if they are to be well adjusted and at low risk for the type of teen problems we see every night on the evening news.

I immediately felt three sets of eyes peering at me as if I was some sort of trash fish—*and I was*. The reality is that I had been trying to be important instead of doing what was important according to God. I was totally out of balance, and my life was in chaos.

During that weekend conference, I got down on my knees and asked God to help me reorder my private world. I went home and sorted out my "in-basket of life."[14]

*Don't ever deny the pain or hurt
you might have to go through, but
always ask, "What can I learn from
it? How can I grow through this?
How can I use it for God's glory?"*

It's All in the Attitude

"Man, does *he* have an attitude!"

"I really like her attitude."

"I don't appreciate your attitude, young man."

Attitude—a common word we use in describing people. It can be positive or negative. I've heard it applied to bass as well: "Now, there's a bass with a real attitude!" As you watch a bass protecting its nest, you end up thinking *that fish has an attitude problem.* When you run into an aggressive fish that smacks the daylight out of your spinner bait, dances on the top of the water, and then throws it back past your ear, you might say, "I like that kind of attitude."

Well, what *is* an attitude? What does it mean? I cheated. I went to the dictionary and found that attitude is "a manner of acting, feeling or thinking that shows one's opinion or disposition." Did you know there's such a thing as a biblical attitude or a mindset that reflects biblical teaching? I've learned quite a bit about this kind of attitude over the years, often during crises.

There have been many unhappy events in my life that I never anticipated. I never expected that an office next to mine would be blown up by a terrorist, injuring and killing people. But it happened.

I never expected a business associate would mismanage my business to the extent that I would almost lose it. But it happened.

I never expected that a high school boy on one of my outings as a youth director would fall off a 400-foot cliff to his death. It happened. I watched as a horse carried him out in a body bag.

I never expected that my daughter at the age of twenty would take a detour in her Christian life and live with boyfriends, use cocaine, and move into alcoholism. But it happened, and continued for four years.

Over the years my wife and I have learned the truth and significance of many passages from God's Word. One passage in particular came alive as we depended on it more and more: "Consider it all joy, my brethren, when you encounter various trials, knowing that the testing of your faith produces endurance" (James 1:2–3 NASB). One verse later, the *Amplified Bible* says, "But let endurance and steadfastness and patience have full play and do a thorough work, so that you may be [people] perfectly and fully developed (with no defects), lacking in nothing."

Learning to put a biblical attitude into practice is a process. The passage from James does not say to "respond this way immediately." You have to feel the pain and grief first, and then you'll be able to consider it all joy.

What does the word *consider* mean? I discovered from commentaries that it refers to an internal attitude of the heart or mind that allows the trials and circumstances of life to affect us either adversely or beneficially. When faced with a problem or challenge, you have the power to consider the situation and decide what your attitude will be. You could say, "This is terrible. Totally upsetting. This is the last thing I want for my life. Why did it have to happen now? Why me?" But the other way to *consider* a problem is to say, "It's not what I wanted or expected, but it happened. There are going to be some difficult times, so how can I make the best of them?"

The verb tense used in the word *consider* indicates a decisiveness of action. It's not an attitude of resignation—"Well, I'll just give up. I'm stuck with this problem. That's the way life is." If you resign yourself, you will sit back and do nothing.

James 1:2–3 calls for us to go against our natural inclination and see trials in life as positives. There will be moments when you'll have to remind yourself, "I think there's a better way of responding to this. Lord, I really want you to help me to see it from a different perspective." With God's help, your mind will shift to a more constructive response. This often takes a lot of work on your part. But discovering the truth of the first few verses in James and in many other passages like it will help you to develop a biblical perspective on life. And that is the ultimate survival tool.

God created us with both the capacity and the freedom to determine how to respond to the unexpected incidents that come our way. You wish a certain event had never occurred, but you can't change the fact that it did. It's a matter of choosing your attitude! Here's how one woman learned this lesson.

> The day had started out rotten. I overslept and was late for work. Everything that happened at the office contributed to my nervous frenzy. By the time I reached the bus stop for my homeward trip, my stomach was one big knot.
>
> As usual, the bus was late, and jammed. I had to stand in the

aisle. As the lurching vehicle pulled me in all directions, my gloom deepened.

Then I heard a deep voice from up front boom, "Beautiful day, isn't it?" Because of the crowd I could not see that man, but I could hear him as he continued to comment on the spring scenery, calling attention to each approaching landmark. This church. That park. This cemetery. That firehouse. Soon all the passengers were gazing out the windows. The man's enthusiasm was so contagious I found myself smiling for the first time that day.

We reached my stop. Maneuvering toward the door, I got a look at our "guide": a plump figure with a black beard, wearing dark glasses and carrying a thin white cane. Incredible! He was blind!

I stepped off the bus, and suddenly, all my built-up tensions drained away. God in His wisdom had sent a blind man to help me see—to see that though there are times when things go wrong, when all seems dark and dreary, it is still a beautiful world. Humming a tune, I raced up the steps to my apartment. I couldn't wait to greet my husband with "Beautiful day, isn't it?" (Source Unknown)

If you've fished much, you've probably run into your share of storms. If you've lived much, you've probably experienced another type of storm—the storms of life. Whether a job loss, illness, accident, divorce, runaway child, or a death, these "storms" can throw us off course and out of our comfort zone. Some penetrate our plans and our life like the attack of an alien invader. No one is immune. I never expected my son to be born profoundly mentally retarded. But he was. I never expected him to die at twenty-two. But he did. Still, my wife and I learned to rest in the sufficiency of Jesus Christ during personal storms. He is sufficient for you, as well.

Praise be to the God and Father of our Lord Jesus Christ, the Father of compassion and the God of all comfort, who comforts us in all our troubles, so that we can comfort those in any trouble with the comfort we ourselves have received from God. (2 Corinthians 1:3–4)

But he said to me, "My grace is sufficient for you, for my power is made perfect in weakness." Therefore I will boast all the more gladly about my weaknesses, so that Christ's power may rest on me. (2 Corinthians 12:9)

When you pass through the waters, I will be with you; and when you pass through the rivers, they will not sweep over you. When you walk through the fire, you will not be burned; the flames will not set you ablaze. (Isaiah 43:2)

*P*ay all your debts except the debt of
love for others—never finish
paying that!

—*Romans* 13:8 TLB

Fishing and Marriage— A Good Mix

18

$\mathcal{A}$re you married? If so, to what? That's right, let's consider "to what" before we consider "to whom."

Fishing and marriage can be a good mix if you work on it. Unfortunately, I've seen some anglers (mostly men) who are married to their fishing. It's on their minds most of the time. It dominates their conversations, and every spare moment is devoted to fishing. Some have even admitted to me that they use fishing to get away from the hassles of their kids and their wife's "honey-do" list. I've seen the hours and energy some men put into the care of their equipment and boat so it doesn't fall into disrepair. I wonder if the same effort has gone into their marriage and family life to keep it from falling into a state of disrepair.

Fishing shouldn't be divisive. It can be unifying and shared by a couple. My wife has always encouraged me to go fishing. Especially when it's a "rougher" trip, such as in the back country of Canada or the Yukon. She's taken up fishing as well and enjoys it. I'd rather fish with Joyce than anyone else—even if it does mean going out later when it's warmer and not staying longer than three hours. We even have matching waders as well as float tubes. Best of all, Joyce caught her first bass this past year (the conversion from trout fishing is happening).

Several years ago, while trout fishing on the Buffalo River in Grand Teton National Park, Joyce's rod bent double. "I've got a big one," she said.

"Oh, you're just stuck on a rock," I replied.

"No, it's a fish."

"No, it's just a rock."

"Norm, rocks don't swim upstream!"

Joyce had me there, and soon she had landed a beautiful 2-pound cutthroat. Joyce wanted me to take a photo of her prized catch before making it that night's dinner. "Why don't you wash it off so it'll look better," she said. "In every fishing picture we have, the fish is bloody and icky."

I agreed. So, getting a viselike grip on the fish, I began to wash him back and forth in the water. That revived him, then he lunged! My grip wasn't enough and he got away. My heart sank to my stomach. I was a dead man!

Now, when a fish gets away like that he's usually long gone. But not this one. "Norm ... look! He's floating downstream. Go fetch him! Quick!" (*Fetch?* That's what I say to my golden retrievers.) Nevertheless, wanting to redeem myself, I went after the floating fish, made a dive for him, missed, and hit the river bottom. As I came up thoroughly soaked, I heard Joyce call out, "Norm, he's still floating. Get him!" This time I ran past the fish along the bank and then walked into the water in order to wait for the fish to float into my hands. When I grabbed it for good, my usually quiet wife began to shout and holler. I think every moose and elk nearby wondered what was going on. Needless to say, Joyce was happy—and I was redeemed. Plus, not only did the lodge cook that fish well, the experience is now a great memory for the two of us. We shared our fishing. I appreciated Joyce's willingness to take up fishing and she appreciated my rescuing her fish (that I'd lost).

Scripture tells us to be like-minded and to live in peace (2 Corinthians 13:11; Romans 14:19). That's what a marriage is about: doing for the other, helping the other, enjoying being together.

There's an interesting concept in marriage that goes a long way in building love and peace in the relationship. It's called the *Relational Bank Account*. Now, you know what you feel like when you've got a surplus in your own personal bank account, right? And you know the result of running in the red, don't you? A Relational Bank Account works the same way.

As is true of any financial account, the Relational Bank Account is in flux because of deposits and withdrawals. Relationship "deposits" vary in size just like our monetary deposits. Every kind word and action adds up, as do very large gifts of love (like retrieving a lost fish!). Withdrawals also vary. A minor disagreement could be a small withdrawal, but a major offense could drain the account. Each spouse needs to be enlightened by the other as to what he or she perceives as a deposit or a withdrawal.

Naturally, the larger the balance, the healthier the relationship. And just like a monetary account, it's best to have sufficient reserves in your Relational Bank Account. Unfortunately, many couples live with their balance at a debit level.

If there is a large balance in the account, a few small withdrawals won't have a big impact. But if the balance is relatively small or hovers around zero, a small withdrawal is definitely felt. The ideal is to keep deposits high and withdrawals low.

What constitutes a relationship deposit for you? For your partner? What is a withdrawal for you? For your spouse? It may help to discuss this before you go fishing the next time![15]

All Scripture is God-breathed and is useful for teaching, rebuking, correcting and training in righteousness, so that the man of God may be thoroughly equipped for every good work.

—2 Timothy 3:16–17

How Do They Grow So Big?

19

$\mathcal{I}$s bigger better? Well, in the search for bass it seems to be. First you want a 5-pounder, then a 10-pounder, then a 15-pounder, and then . . . the world record! This is especially true when a company like SpiderWire offers $100,000 for a world-record bass (if caught on one of their products).

So, what is considered a large bass? Some pros say a 5- or 6-pounder qualifies. A trophy bass is even larger, but again opinions vary. The Florida Department of Fishery says a 10-pounder would make the grade. In California, biologists and anglers agree that a 10-pound fish is big, but a 12-pounder is a real trophy!

How do you find big bass and catch them? Reading the many articles and books, you end up with the same insights. Big bass are efficient in using their energy. That's how they get big. They find a home where they have little intrusion, plenty of food, and shelter.

They don't want to move around a lot for their food. And deep water, or access to deep water, is a must. They can be at home anywhere from 8- to 30-feet down.

If you're after big bass, use big baits. When they look for food, they want big crawdads, big bluegill, big trout, or crappie, or shad. A 2-inch minnow isn't a mouthful. Bass can eat forage fish up to one-third of their length. A 4-pound, 20-inch bass can eat a 7-inch shad or trout. There's a whole new series of large baits, from the 8- or 9-inch Castaic trout baits to the 10-inch Basstrix trout baits. Watch out, though. You may want to pump iron for a few weeks before throwing one of these all day.

Where have the largest (trophy) bass been caught? The January/February 1999 issue of *Bass West* magazine listed the twenty-five biggest bass of all time. As I studied the list I was amazed. The fish ranged from a 22-pound, 4-ounce giant caught in Alabama in 1932 to an 18-pound, 10-ounce bass. In second place was a 22-pound, 1-ounce fish caught at Castaic Lake, California, in 1991. Of the top twenty-five, twenty-one were caught in California! And eight of those came from Castaic Lake! *Why so many in California? And why so many at Castaic Lake?* It's the food. These lakes are stocked with rainbow trout—practically a government subsidized weight-gain program for bass. I've seen bass chase 14-inch trout. I've seen bass attack caught-trout being kept in a wire basket. Bass grow large because of what they take into their big mouth. And trout are a great food source.

What's your food source? And I don't mean for your body. What feeds your heart and your mind? For many people, it's television, the Internet, or what they hear from others. These resources are readily available, and sometimes you do find something that's worth taking in. But another food source is even better. It's the Bible, the Word of God.

Unfortunately, some people develop a form of anorexia when it comes to reading the Scriptures. They have an aversion to consuming the Word of God. We may believe in the Bible, but if we aren't feeding on it we become spiritually undernourished.

There's one answer to this problem: eat—feed on God's Word. Jesus himself said, "Man shall not live by bread alone, but on every word that proceeds from the mouth of God" (Matthew 4:4 NKJV).

$\mathcal{D}$o not be conformed to this world but be transformed by the renewal of your mind.

—*Romans 12:2* RSV

A Matter of Degrees

Do you pay much attention to the temperature? I do, especially as I get older. I don't like it as cold as I used to during the winter, especially if the wind picks up. Thirty degrees is all right, but not with a twenty-mile-an-hour wind.

The more I got into bass fishing the more conscious I became of water temperatures. Bass are sensitive to water temperature changes. You can be picking up bass regularly in your favorite spot, but have a front come through dropping the water temperature a couple of degrees and the bite stops. Your presentation is the same. Your line selection, which had been so hot, is the same, so it's not you. Mr. Bass just didn't like the temperature change.

I've read about the "strike window" of bass. This refers to the distance a bass will move to get his food. Naturally, your lure needs to be in the strike window if you want any success. Think of the strike window as a balloon on the snout of a bass that expands or deflates based on the activity of the fish. Cold water is one factor that shrinks the strike window.[16]

I fish a high mountain lake primarily for smallmouth, but a few largemouth are there, as well. I constantly read water temperature reports or check the water myself. Why? I've learned that when the water is 53 degrees, there's no action. When it's 54 degrees, still none. But for some reason, in this lake, when it hits 55 degrees, they're on the prowl and looking to feed.

Jimmy Houston has a helpful hint regarding water temperatures. He suggests that when temperatures go down, so do the fish. Not only that, they move slower. He also suggests there's a key water temperature  for bass fishing—58 degrees. For some reason bass seem to move more at this temperature. And it doesn't matter whether it's on the way up or down either. In the spring when the water temperature hits this level, bass move into prespawning staging areas. But watch out for the drop-off in activity that occurs in nighttime temperatures. You may do well during the afternoon, but during the morning you may not get a bite since the temperature fell two or three degrees. It will take a couple of hours of sun to get them cranked up again.[17]

Temperature is a big part of fishing. It's important in our life, as well. If your body temperature is at 96 or 100 degrees instead of 98.6 or what's normal for you, you may have a problem.

But let me ask a question that's a bit personal. How's your spiritual temperature? I've heard people described as "on fire for the Lord." I've also heard comments like, "That guy is really lukewarm in his faith." How would people describe your faith?

Sometimes people's faith is affected by their environment. It doesn't need to be. Our faith can be strong and consistent if we're in close contact with Jesus Christ. That's the way to keep our spiritual temperature up there. The more we distance ourselves from Him, the more lethargic we get, like a bass in cold water. I'd rather be an active, warm believer, and I hope you would, too.

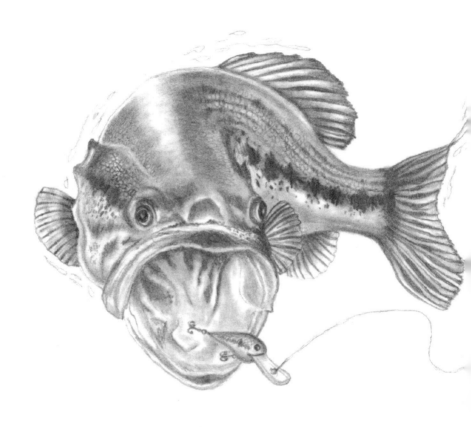

Check the Label

21

$\mathcal{L}$et's face it, bass anglers are into labels. I was walking a shoreline at a small lake looking for some belligerent bass when a boat pulled in. The guy was excited. He wanted to show off his new Phoenix rod (he emphasized the brand name several times). I had to admit, it was a beauty. It had flexibility as well as backbone.

Listen to anglers when they get together and talk about rods. You hear names like Bionic Blade, All-Star, Daiwa, Shakespeare Ugly Stick, Berkley, Shimano, and Loomis. Watch how shoppers look over equipment in the fishing section. As long as it's got the "right" name—the right label—they're satisfied.

Labels. They're on everything today. We're told to "check the label" to make sure it's the real deal. When shopping for clothes one of the first things many people look at is the label. We select certain foods in the market based on the label. Labels are a major part of life. Indeed, we label people.

It's interesting how quickly labels are given to children. In the first few months Mom or Dad will say, "He's more alert at this age than she was." Or, "She's so easygoing compared to him." Of course, labels aren't always a good thing. Some people go through their entire lives burdened by an undeserved label of "slow," "inept," "stupid," "irresponsible," "loser," you name it. Labels, if they stick, are like an ointment rubbed onto the skin. In time it penetrates deeper. A label becomes part of a person's perception of himself.

I've heard anglers put themselves down when they're having an off day. One man said, "Well, I'm such a klutz that I can't even figure out this new reel." It's as if someone wrote this word on a tag and attached it to his chest, defining and determining everything that happens to him for the rest of his life. As a therapist I've seen hundreds of people struggle with being branded in this way. Labels on products are good. I do want to see a Quantum label on a reel before I select it, but labels on a person?

During the Vietnam War, a mobile army surgical hospital (M.A.S.H.) would prepare for incoming helicopters and their loads of wounded and dying soldiers by using a system of triage to categorize the wounded by the severity of their injuries. A tag with a certain color was placed on the dying to indicate they could not be saved. They were hopeless. They would not recover. A second colored tag was used for those with superficial wounds. They would receive medical attention and would recover. A third colored tag was placed on those who were in critical condition but could make it with medical care. They might recover.

A critically wounded man was brought to one mobile hospital, and after examination he was tagged "dying—will not recover." He was given a painkiller and left to die. A nurse came by, though, saw he was conscious, and began to talk with him. After a while she felt he could probably make it. So she reached down, took off the tag, and replaced it with one that indicated he could recover. Because she changed that tag, he's alive today.

What about you? Is there any possibility that you're going through life with the wrong tag? How do you see yourself? Critical and unsalvageable, or do you have hope for yourself? If you have a label on you, who placed it there? Was it someone in your family? Could you have been the one who put it there?

The tag God puts on you indicates "salvageable," "redeemable," "valuable." Those are great labels aren't they?[18]

God has declared us to be adequate
because of what He has done for us
through Jesus Christ.

Perfectly Adequate

22

I'm all for neatness. I like order and structure. It helps to know where everything is when you're out there fishing. You don't have to waste time trying to remember, *Now, where did I put that. . . ?* Sometimes when the bass are in a feeding frenzy and you're changing lures or have to put on new hooks, you start tossing stuff into the tackle box or onto the floor of the boat. That happens. Usually you sort it out later. Unfortunately, I've fished with some who haven't sorted it out for years.

I've seen some anglers go overboard (no pun intended) on this neatness stuff, though. Everything has to be perfect. And I mean perfect! One guy told us what kind of shoes or boots we could wear in his boat and what kind we couldn't. He didn't want his carpeting to get scuffed up. Equipment needs to be cared for and kept up, but I've seen some worry more over keeping it showroom quality than enjoying its usage. There is no balance. They are perfectionists.

Perfectionism is a mental monster. It rages and steals the satisfaction out of life. Do you know any perfectionists? They strive to do the impossible and expect it from others. The standards they set for themselves and for others are ... well, forget it! No one could consistently attain to them.

The drive to be perfect brings with it a strange companion—a high degree of sensitivity to failure. The pain of failure—of doing less than our absolute best—is much greater for perfectionists because they have unrealistic standards. The greater the distance between performance and standards, the higher the degree of pain. Ouch. You may have seen this in your family or your friends or. . . . You're not one of these people, are you?

Perfectionists have a pet statement: "It could always be better." Things are never good enough—even when they're outstanding. Perfectionists seem to live with tapes inside their heads that continuously play the same old message: "It isn't good enough. I must be perfect. If I do better, I'll get some approval. Try harder, but don't make a mistake." And this message is often conveyed to others around them, as well.

Perfectionists live by many unspoken rules that have a powerful influence on their lives. These rules create tremendous stress in themselves and others. Three of the most common are:

- I must never make a mistake.
- I must never fail.
- I must play it safe so I always succeed.

Perfectionists are also procrastinators. They don't want to try unless they know they'll be successful. So the job is put off again and again.

Perfectionism isn't attainable. We are who we are because of what God has done for us. He calls us to live a life of *excellence*. Here's the difference between the pursuer of excellence and the perfectionist: The perfectionist reaches for impossible goals, whereas the pursuer of excellence enjoys meeting high standards that are within his reach.

The perfectionist bases his value of himself upon his accomplishments, while the person who pursues excellence values himself simply for who he is. The perfectionist tends to remember his past mistakes and dwells on them. He is convinced that everyone else remembers them, too. The pursuer of excellence, on the other hand, will correct his mistakes, learn the lessons they have to offer, and then forget about them.

Let's face it, we'll never be perfect here on earth, and perfectionism is not a spiritual calling or gift either. Perfectionists strive to be "adequate," but they never reach their goal!

Adequacy is a free gift to us and always has been. Any shortage in our lives has been paid for by God's free gift—Jesus Christ. We can get loose of the criterion of human performance because God calls us to be faithful. This is His standard—faithfulness!

"Whoever can be trusted with very little can also be trusted with much" (Luke 16:10).

"But the fruit of the Spirit is . . . faithfulness" (Galatians 5:22).

When you're stressed, you're like a
rubber band that's being stretched.
When the pressure is released, it
returns to normal. But if stretched
too much for too long, it begins to
lose its elasticity, develops cracks, then
eventually breaks.

All Stressed Up With Nowhere to Go?

23

*Y*our muscles begin to quiver. Your fingers start tapping. You sense your eye is about to twitch. You can feel your heartbeat intensifying and your blood pressure rising as your schedule summons you to action. You rush to the bass pro shop to grab some on-sale items, pick up the dry cleaning, snag some fast (junk) food for the drive, get the trailer fixed, return three phone calls, and then . . . then comes "great" news! Guess who's dropping in to stay with you for the next week? (You fill in the blank for this one.) Just what you need. Now that you feel tighter than a rubber band and your guts are twisted like a pretzel, what do you have? A classic case of twenty-first-century stress.

Stress is a common, catchall word used to describe the tension and pressure felt in overwhelming situations. More to the point, it's irritation brought on by *any* bothersome situation. The Latin word for stress is *strictus*, meaning "to be drawn tight." Stress is anything that places conflicting or heavy demands upon you. Does this describe the pattern of your life?

For most people, fishing offers a chance to de-stress. You get on the water, fill your lungs with fresh air, flip that plastic or crankbait out there, and with any luck, your line tightens. Suddenly your stress does a vanishing act. Unfortunately, I've seen bass anglers carry their stress with them right into the boat. And when their reel fouls up with a backlash for the eighth time in a row, or they hang their spinner bait in the brush again and again, what happens to their stress level? Or, what about the anglers in a tournament who are dead set on winning and start fishing faster and faster and faster?

Every rubber band can tolerate a different amount of pressure before it snaps. People also have varying tolerance levels. What's stressful to one person may not be stressful to another. Some get stressed about what's coming up in the future; others after the fact. Some people have been stretched so long and so often they've become brittle. They crumble or explode at the slightest irritation. So where's all this stress stuff coming from? From the hassles and upsets of life, right?

Actually, most stress comes from within—from wrapping feelings, thoughts, and attitudes around more than we were built for. That's right, our inner responses are the culprits. What we put into our minds and think about affects our bodies.

How's your thought life? What do you think about on the drive to the lake? What is on your mind out on the water? What is the first thing you listen to on the radio in the morning? What is the last TV program you watch before attempting to sleep at night? Your answers may expose the reason for some of the stress you feel.

A stressful situation is intensified by how we talk to ourselves during the crisis. *This is awful. This shouldn't be happening. I can't be late. How will I get all this stuff done? I can't believe I lost that 10-pounder!* The more negative and angry our thoughts, the more stressed we become.

So how are you feeling right now? Relaxed? Uptight? As you think about the issues facing you today, what's your stress level? If you're feeling stressed, read Psalm 23. This psalm serves as the Good Shepherd's eviction notice to every stressful thought that might take up residence in your head. Read Psalm 23 aloud each day for a month. I use some of my alone time fishing to memorize Scripture, and it keeps me from thoughts that could ruin my fishing day. Who knows? It may work for you, too.

> He refreshes and restores my life—my self; He leads me in the paths of righteousness [uprightness and right standing with Him—not for my earning it, but] for His name's sake. Yes, though I walk through the [deep, sunless] valley of the shadow of death, I will fear or dread no evil, for You are with me; Your rod [to protect] and Your staff [to guide], they comfort me. (Psalm 23:3–4 AMP)

It is senseless for you to work so hard from early morning until late at night, fearing you will starve to death; for God wants his loved ones to get their proper rest.

—Psalm 127:2 TLB

Hurried and Hassled

24

Hectic, hurried, and hassled. Ever have one of those days when you just couldn't stop for a minute for fear you'd be run over? You know—the kind of day when all the circumstances kept shoving you from behind, pushing you so intensely that it was all you could do to keep from stumbling over your own two feet.

On one of those days it seems that everyone and everything wants a piece of you. If you hesitate for a moment, you'll be devoured. You feel frantic, like a chipmunk running around an exercise wheel, going faster and faster but going nowhere.

Have you ever asked, "Will it never end? Where will I find more time? What else can go wrong? How can I hurry up to hurry more?" With commitments to family, spouse, work, church, and who knows what else, it's easy to push our personal accelerator to the floor and move faster and faster. Unfortunately, this happens on the water as well. I've seen

- anglers hurrying down the docks and either tripping and sprawling on the dock or (literally) missing the boat. (You don't want to be around when this soaked angler cuts loose!)
- boats tearing by at 70-plus miles per hour when there's no tournament to be concerned over.
- an angler dragging his plastic worm so fast it's practically smoking! (Worms aren't runners, they're crawlers!)
- a guy in a boat next to me racing to change his rig, but the faster he goes the more that Palomar knot refuses to cooperate.

It's easy for hurry to turn into frantic. Frantic people are difficult to be around, even if they are Christians. And as Christians we are not called to live like this. Consider Tim Hansel's words:

> We are called to be faithful, not frantic. If we are to meet the challenges of today, there must be integrity between our words and our lives, and more reliance on the source of our purpose.
>
> "Unless the Lord builds the house, they labor in vain who build it; Unless the Lord guards the city, the watchman stays awake in vain. It is vain for you to rise up early, to sit up late, to eat the bread of sorrows; for so He gives His beloved sleep" (Psalm 127:1–2 NKJV).
>
> Almost all Christianity reveals itself in feverish work, excessive hurry, and exhaustion. I believe the enemy has done an effective job of convincing us that unless a person is worn to a frazzle, running here and there, he or she cannot possibly be a dedicated, sacrificing, spiritual Christian. Perhaps the Seven Deadly Sins have recruited another member—Overwork.
>
> We need to remember that our strength lies not in hurried efforts and ceaseless long hours, but in our quietness and confidence. The world today says, "Enough is not enough." Christ

answers softly, "Enough is enough."[19]

Hurrying isn't the answer. It won't help. It won't work. It will only stress you out more and build a sense of panic. So what can you do? Slow down. This advice may sound paradoxical, but when your day is coming apart and you're running around in circles, stop. Hold everything. Sit down in a comfortable chair, take a deep breath, and read the following prayer (slowly):

> Steady my hurried pace with a vision of the eternal reach of time.
>
> Give me, amid the confusion of the day, the calmness of the everlasting hills.
>
> Break the tensions of my nerves and muscles with the soothing music of the singing streams that live in my memory.
>
> Teach me the art of taking minute vacations—of slowing down to look at a flower, to chat with a friend, to pat a dog, to smile at a child, to read a few lines from a good book.
>
> Slow me down, Lord, and inspire me to send my roots deep into the soil of life's enduring values, that I may grow toward my greater destiny.
>
> Remind me each day that the race is not always to the swift; that there is more to life than increasing its speed.
>
> Let me look upward to the towering oak and know that it grew great and strong because it grew slowly and well.[20]

It's not what's in your head that counts, it's what's in your heart and what you do.

Technique vs. Results

You gotta have the right technique. You can't just heave that spinner bait out there. And when you're flippin' those plastic worms into the brush and under those docks, this is how you hold your line in one hand and your rod in the other. The rod should be at a 45-degree angle. Your hand holding it should be relaxed and parallel to the water. Take the line near the reel with your other hand and pull it out about an arm's length. Your bait needs to be at the length of the rod. You're ready. Dip your rod, swing your bait forward, follow with the other hand and let the line slide out easily. Remember you're not throwing your line, you're using your wrist.

Now, when it comes to setting the hook, pull the rod toward your shoulder. It doesn't matter which shoulder, just make sure it's not just straight up with your arms away from your body. Use an offset hook set because there's more power when your arms are close to your body.[21]

The above is what is meant by technique. I've watched anglers who make "technique" look so simple. It seems to be a part of them. I've seen others who talk about technique incessantly and have all the right moves and skills. They've practiced their casting skills for hours. They've honed them to perfection. They've got the technique, but there's only one problem. I don't see them catching anything.

Skills for most sports, whether fishing, hunting, basketball, or baseball, are built on proper technique. Take baseball, for example: Players spend hours trying to master their hitting technique. They work on getting the bat off their shoulder at the proper time, keeping their head down, stepping into the ball, using the strength of their legs, keeping their swing level. Hours go into mustering the proper form. But it won't make any difference in the score of the game or the amount of the player's salary unless he does one thing—hit the ball consistently. Technique is one thing, results are another.

Theology is the same way. You may know some guy whose theology is exacting and correct. He can quote chapter and verse for his belief as well as the doctrines of John Calvin and Martin Luther. But unless this theology is translated into something else, it's not worth much. What you and I believe is important, but not as much as who we are as a person and the way we behave.

You can have correct theology, but no joy.

You can have correct theology, but no peace.

You can have correct theology, but no self-control.

If that's the case, what good is your theology?

> But the fruit of the Spirit is love, joy, peace, patience, kindness, goodness, faithfulness, gentleness and self-control. Against such things there is no law. (Galatians 5:22–23)

Correct theology by itself won't draw others to the Lord, but the fruit of the Spirit will. What others see in you has more impact than what you tell them you believe.

In baseball it's easy to have a good technique and still strike out. In bass fishing it's easy to have a good technique and not catch anything. It's the same with our faith. If you're striking out, it's time for a change, isn't it?[22]

We're not self-sufficient. We'll make mistakes. They're a part of life. When you're in a jam, admit it and ask for help.

Not Going Anywhere

26

*M*y daughter Sheryl and I were in the boat together. Before going out that morning, the owner of the lodge had gone over a map with us showing the best bays and areas to fish. She also pointed out various shoals and rocks to avoid so we wouldn't rip out the bottom of the boat. Then we were off to fish.

We cranked up that 10-horse motor, headed out of the bay, and took a right turn. We were going full speed (not exactly the same as a 20-foot Ranger with a 225 Merc pushing it along) when we suddenly came to a grinding stop. That is, the boat stopped but we didn't. We both lunged forward about a foot. We weren't hurt, just surprised.

"Whoa, where'd that come from?" Sheryl asked. "Didn't you see it?"

"Me? If I'd seen it we wouldn't have hit it. You're in the front of the boat. How come you didn't see it?"

"I was looking around, not down."

So there we were. We looked over the side and quickly saw that we were firmly aground a big rock. We decided to try rocking the boat, but we barely moved. The problem was, we needed to back off the rock, not go side-to-side, and the motor wasn't going to help any. We were stuck. Just then a boat came around the bend carrying Sheryl's husband, Bill, and my cousin-in-law, Ken.

"Oh no," I said. "We can't let them know we're stuck. We'll never hear the end of it. Plus, they've got the video camera."

Sheryl replied, "Quick, start casting. We'll just act as though we stopped here to fish. They'll never know."

We whipped out our rods and let those Daredevil lures fly toward shore. It wasn't a very likely place for the pike to hang out, but we were busy "fishing." As the other boat approached, we heard lots of laughter. We turned around and saw them getting closer, with the video camera taking it all in.

Trying gamely to keep up the act, Sheryl shouted across the water, "Hey, we haven't caught anything big yet. Why waste the video?" (More laughter.)

"Who are you trying to kid," replied Bill. "You're not fishing. You're stuck high and dry on a rock."

"Us?"

"Yeah, you."

"How could you tell?"

They said they had heard the crunch, and then after seeing us, they knew no boat would be at an angle like ours if it wasn't on a rock. The long and short of it was, we had to admit what had happened plus ask for help to get off the rock. No damage was done to the boat—just our egos, especially when we later viewed the video and heard their commentary.

Fortunately, this wasn't the only unusual experience of the day. The next one happened just fifteen minutes later. It wasn't a great experience, it was *fantastic!* We were fishing a shoreline that had an abundance of reeds and growth on top of the water. Sheryl saw an open spot and flipped her topwater lure right in the middle. A second later the water rippled and something sucked that popper right out of sight. The battle was on. Her reel was screaming. The day before she had broken off two good-sized fish because the drag had been too tight. I loosened it, but now worried that I had loosened it too much. This time the problem wasn't the reel, it was the fish. The third time it went past the boat we saw it. We were speechless. It was the largest pike we'd ever seen.

It came closer and I reached out to net it while Sheryl yelled, "Be careful. Don't lose it." It was too big for the net so I reached out and sort of folded it in. We landed it. Sheryl was screaming, and I was yelling.

Bill and Ken were fishing a half-mile away. Apparently Bill looked at Ken and said, "I recognize that yell. Sheryl's got a big fish. Let's get over there."

This time we didn't mind at all when they approached with the video camera cranking. We weighed the fish, took pictures, and released it. Twenty-two pounds! The largest caught in Uchi Lake that year and the eighth-largest released in that province of Canada that year as well.

Reflecting on the experience, Sheryl said, "If we had stayed stuck on the rock, I'd never have caught that fish. In fact, if Bill and Ken hadn't come by we'd probably still be stuck."

Have there been times in your life when you felt like you were stuck on a rock but wouldn't admit it? It's the same feeling as getting your car stuck in the mud and then tromping the accelerator for all it's worth but all your wheels do is spin and sink deeper.

Two things in life will help. First, when you're in trouble and not moving forward, admit you need help. It's all right. Proverbs says,

> Be not wise in your own eyes. (3:7 AMP)
>
> Do you see a man wise in his own eyes and conceit? There is more hope for a [self-confident] fool than for him. (26:12 AMP)
>
> Where there is no counsel, purposes are frustrated, but with many counselors they are accomplished. (15:22 AMP)

Second, to avoid getting into difficult situations, watch where you're going. Be watchful about decisions you make. Be watchful about what you think, what you say, and the course you take in life. Above all, "Watch over your heart with all diligence" (Proverbs 4:23 NASB).

Sometimes the reason we aren't catching those bass is because we're missing the mark. But a small adjustment could make a big difference. The same's true for the rest of life.

Successful Failures

27

Over the years I've seen my share of discouraged anglers—usually down because they aren't catching bass when others are. After trying old and new approaches and baits, they begin to wonder, *What's wrong with me? What am I doing wrong?* I, too, can remember dry spells.

In his great book *Bass Master Shaw Grigsby—Notes on Fishing and Life*, Shaw points out that when you decided to become a bass fisherman, you selected a sport that has the potential to humiliate you. Even the best pro-anglers have off days. And these men and women know what it's all about.

A failure or mistake—in any endeavor—carries with it the opportunity to make a course correction to get us back on the right track. Those who stick with it have learned this lesson. They've got a never-give-up attitude.

Remember the voice of Mufasa, the father lion in *The Lion King*, or the voice of Darth Vader in the *Star Wars* films? The voice behind those characters was that of James Earl Jones. You might also remember his role in *Field of Dreams*. He's won three Emmy Awards, two Tonys, a Golden Globe, and a Grammy.

Success hasn't always come easy for James Earl Jones. At the age of fourteen he stuttered so much that he never spoke in class. He was awkward, shy, and a loner. The trauma of a family move had created such insecurity for him that he found it difficult to talk without stuttering. He began to communicate through notes.

One day his teacher asked James to read a poem out loud in front of the class. It took courage, but as he read, the words started to flow. He liked reading aloud and wanted to do more, so he practiced over and over. Eventually, his speaking ability led to wins in competitions and a college scholarship. For years he did small roles in off-Broadway productions and supported himself as a janitor. Through it all, James never, never gave up. And he says those early disappointments and failures taught him much and played a major role in who he is today.[23]

Failure will touch everyone's life at some time. We can either live behind our failures or beyond them. Let's look at some heroes who have lived beyond them.

Have you ever fallen flat on your face? Probably. But have you done it on cold, hard ice—in front of millions? Probably not. Speed skater Dan Jansen did. He fell not only in the 1988 Olympics but also in the 1992 Olympics. Then in the 1994 Olympics, his last shot at Olympic glory, he leaned a bit too far and brushed his hands on the ice, costing him a medal. He had one last event to skate in—the 1,000-meter race. It wasn't really his specialty event. He didn't feel good, and seven competitors had already recorded better times than his in preliminary races. But in his last Olympic race he won! And he won it in a world-record time. Dan Jansen wouldn't give up. He didn't allow discouragement to rule him.

Alexander Fleming was a research physician who made a mistake one day. He left a window open and some mold blew in and contaminated bacteria culture in a dish. He could have thrown his hands up in frustration and discarded the contaminated dish. Instead, he decided to see if anything would happen to the bacteria. Something did! The mold produced a substance that prevented staphylococcus growth. He named the substance penicillin. It has healed millions. A mistake? Yes. A failure? Not in this case.

As you go through life, try to grow and learn from your failures. Failures remind us that we are not God! And sometimes we need this reminder. It's when we feel ordinary that God can use us the most. Failure can be God's tool to get our attention when we're stuck and need to move on. It can be the instrument He uses to pry us out of our comfort zone.

Failure is an ingredient for success. Many successful people have said the key to making good decisions in their lives came from making bad ones.[24]

So, consider this question: What can you do to reconstruct the way you view failure? Remember the words of Paul?

> I don't mean to say I am perfect. I haven't learned all I should even yet, but I keep working toward the day when I will finally be all that Christ saved me for and wants me to be. No, dear brothers, I am still not all I should be but I am bringing all my energies to bear on this one thing: Forgetting the past and looking forward to what lies ahead, I strain to reach the end of the race and receive the prize for which God is calling us up to heaven because of what Christ Jesus did for us. (Philippians 3:12–14 TLB)

*D*o not let the sun go down on your
anger [resentment or bitterness].

—*Ephesians 4:26* RSV

Controlling Anger Before It Controls You

28

Jim Grassi tells the story of Hank Parker:

Even as a teenager, Hank Parker was hung up on fishing. He remembers a fishing trip to Lake Wylie, on the border of the Carolinas, where he literally got "hung up." It was an overcast afternoon in February, and fishing had been slow for the seventeen-year-old. He had spent most of the day carefully working a crankbait around some old submerged stumps at the mouth of a creek. As his deep-diving plug was biting into the muddy bottom, Hank suddenly felt a tug. Below the surface a fish quickly wrapped Hank's line around a root and refused to move. Hank bowed his back and mustered all his strength to pull his lure free. Suddenly the root broke, and the frustrated angler began to reel in his lure. He fully expected that the bass had long since freed itself from the snag and swum to safer waters.

When he lifted the tangle of dead limbs out of the water, however, Hank was surprised to find that the huge bass was still hooked! "I think the old fish was taking its last bite when he hit my lure," remembers Hank. "The crankbait looked like a crappie jig in his large mouth, and he wasn't fighting at all."

Now many years later, Hank found himself "hung up" again. This time, it was at the World's Fair Fishing Tournament in Knoxville, Tennessee. He needed just one more fish to clinch a victory when he hooked a monster, a beautiful 8- or 9-pound fish that could have won it all for him. Unfortunately, it got tangled up in a discarded trout line and some brush. He carefully maneuvered the boat over to the snag and began reeling. But as he reached down to grab the fish, the tangled bass slipped away from him. So did $50,000 in prize money. Of course Hank felt a momentary flash of anger, but he didn't let it settle in.[25]

When I read about Hank, I thought, *He's really got his act together.* I've seen guys stay angry for days over something trivial. I've also heard them a quarter-mile away on the lake, sounding as though something or someone was going to be destroyed.

A few years ago a book titled *Anger Kills* was published. A strong title, but unfortunately, true. Anger when out of control can kill you. The emotion prepares your body for action. Did you know that when you're angry your blood clots much more quickly, additional adrenaline is released into your bloodstream, and your muscles tense up? Your blood pressure can increase from 130 to 230, and your heart beats faster—often up to 230 beats per minute or higher. People have had strokes and heart attacks during anger fits because of the increased blood pressure, even over a fishing mishap.

When anger is not released, your body remains ready for action. Your heart continues to beat rapidly, blood pressure continues to rise, and blood chemicals fluctuate. The results *can* harm you physically. And these are only the physical symptoms of anger.

Unreleased anger also has emotional and spiritual consequences. It turns into resentment—the desire for revenge. But the anger hurts the one who carries it far more than the one who is the object of it.

Dr. S. I. McMillen's book, *None of These Diseases*, tells the story of Dale Carnegie's visit to Yellowstone National Park. Observing the grizzly bears feeding, a guide told Carnegie that the grizzly bear could whip any animal in the West with the exception of the buffalo and the Kodiak bear. That very night as people sat watching a grizzly eat, they noticed the grizzly would allow only one animal to eat with him—a skunk. Of course, the grizzly could have beaten the skunk in any fight. He probably resented the skunk and wanted to get even with it for coming into his own feeding domain. But he didn't attack the skunk. Why? Because he knew the high cost of getting even! It wouldn't be worth it.

Look at the result of anger in the life of a man in the Old Testament. His name was Nabal. David sent some of his men to Nabal, who was a very wealthy man. Although they needed some food, Nabal basically told them to get lost. When David heard this, he gathered his men together and set out to fight Nabal. But Abigail, Nabal's wife, heard what her husband had done. So she gathered a large amount of food, went out to meet them, and appeased David and his men with her gift. This is how Scripture describes what happened next:

> And Abigail came to Nabal; and behold, he was holding a feast in his house like the feast of a king; and his heart was merry, for he was very drunk; so she told him nothing at all until the morning light. But in the morning, when the wine was gone out of Nabal, and his wife told him these things, his heart died within him, and he became [paralyzed, helpless as] a stone. And about ten days after that, the Lord smote Nabal and he died. (1 Samuel 25:36–38 AMP)

The phrase "his heart died within him" could mean Nabal had a stroke or a heart attack. Why did this happen? Nabal probably reacted to his wife's actions with intense anger. Something to think about the next time you're angry!

*If the Lord delights in a man's way,
he makes his steps firm; though he
stumble, he will not fall, for the Lord
upholds him with his hand.*

—Psalm 37:23–24

Shortcuts to Nowhere

29

We've all taken shortcuts in life. We think there's a better and more efficient way to do things. Sometimes we call it being creative, being inventive, or being a pioneer. We definitely avoid terms like lazy or nonconformist, though there could be some truth in all of these words at one time or another.

Several years ago (before I saw the light and discovered bass fishing) a friend and I were wading the upper part of the Buffalo River in Grand Teton National Park, fishing for the Yellowstone cutthroat. After catching and releasing several fish and walking and wading about two miles, we were ready to take a break and get some food.

My fishing partner Gary is a unique individual. He's one of the leading psychologists in the country and director of a marriage and family center for a leading Christian university. He has studied in Europe, is a card-carrying magician (sometimes I'd like to make him disappear), and has gone on two archeological expeditions looking for the Ark on Mount Ararat in Turkey. Those are just some of his credentials. What I haven't mentioned yet is that he's a loose cannon. You never know what he's going to do or say.

Walking upstream we came to a bend in the river. I decided to take a shortcut across and save a few yards. Bad decision. As I got closer to the opposite shore the water stopped being water and turned into mud—a thick, sticky, dense, quicksand-type of sludge. I got stuck, and I mean stuck. I didn't want to get my equipment full of that stuff, so without thinking I said, "Gary, here, take my rod and the video camera." Another bad decision. Then I said, "Gary, I need some help." He answered, "Right..." with a tone that told me I was in *really* deep mud. He grinned, lifted the video camera, and pressed the "on" button. Me? I was looking for his "off" button to punch.

"Wiggle your legs, Norm, so the folks at home can see what you're in!" (Later when I watched the video, I was kind of shocked to see what I was stuck in. Had I been there by myself, I'd probably still be there!). I wiggled and felt myself sink another two inches.

"Dumb idea, Gary, real dumb."

Gary said, "Hey, guy, let me give you a hand," and with that he began to clap. After a lot of bantering, pleading, making vain and ludicrous promises, selling my birthright, and promising to let him out-fish me the rest of my life, he tossed me a log. I climbed on and promptly fell off. I had a weird look on my face. I know. The camera captured it all.

The last scene on the video is me finding a firm foothold and charging up the bank at the cameraman, and then all you see is the sky and trees. We've had more fun showing that video in seminars all over the country. It's a great illustration of what can happen when you try to take a shortcut. It's also a sobering reminder of what it feels like to be stuck. When you're immobilized like that you feel hopeless. Some people feel like that in life. They feel stuck in their job, their family, their marriage, their illness. And some of them don't have a good friend around to help sort it out. Perhaps you can identify with some of these statements:

- Being stuck is setting goals but putting off doing anything to make them a reality.
- Being stuck is wanting everything to be perfect before taking a step.
- Being stuck is making a promise to yourself, to God, or to someone else and not keeping it.
- Being stuck is not taking steps to keep yourself from physical or emotional harm—or perhaps continuing to be a victim.
- Being stuck is waiting until things become so unbearable that you just can't take any more.
- Being stuck is allowing the fear of failure, disappointment, or change to keep you from taking the risk to change. Sometimes we don't take God at His word because He doesn't come through the way we expect.
- Being stuck is the inability to see various alternatives that do exist.
- Being stuck is feeling helpless, frustrated, worthless, and hopeless.
- Being stuck is seeing life through a negative filter and expecting the worst from situations and people.
- Being stuck is underestimating the potential that God has given to you.
- Being stuck can be minimizing your situation, condition, or problem—in other words, being in denial.

- Becoming and remaining stuck is a detour from blessing that may end up becoming a permanent route for the rest of your life. It bypasses all that God has for us. Regrets do this to us. [26]

If you're stuck in the mud by a river, I can't help you much. But if you're stuck in some area of your life, God's Word *can* help. Remember: " 'For I know the plans I have for you,' declares the Lord, 'plans to prosper you and not to harm you, plans to give you hope and a future' " (Jeremiah 29:11).

*Blessed are your eyes,
because they see.*

—Matthew 13:16 NASB

What Do You See?

30

$\mathcal{S}$ight fishing is one of the ways to catch bass. In a way it's a combination of two sports: hunting and fishing. You're involving hunting because you're looking for a fish that at first you may not see. This involves stalking as well. You look for telltale signs like a shadow or a swirl, not just a bass protecting its bed. You have to move carefully since a bass notices the smallest movement.

Recently I read an article in *Bassin'* on the value of sunglasses for sight fishing, especially the value of polarization to eliminate glare. When it comes to sunglasses, it's not a simple choice. The article described the differences and value of various colors of lenses. Some seem better than others for distinguishing the contrast between a rock and a bass. Seeing fish in the water is better with amber lenses rather than gray. One expert suggested that Vermilion is the best all-around lens because it increases the contrast more than other colors.

It also blocks more blue light than gray, which helps with focusing and visual activity. Once you read articles like this you begin checking your old sunglasses—and then the prices of new ones (if you have prescription lenses, they're even more expensive).

When it comes to sight fishing from the shoreline, I've found the ultimate answer: Sheffield. That's right, Sheffield. Now you're wondering, *What's a Sheffield?* It's not a what, it's a who. Sheffield is one of my golden retrievers. I use him as a bass spotter—a "shoreline sonar." I never intended to, it just happened.

In 1984, for our twenty-fifth wedding anniversary, Joyce and I had our backyard redone to look like the mountains. It's a small area, but it has a couple of birch, a couple of liquid amber trees, and a pine. We also put in some small ponds with a recirculating waterfall for sound and aeration. Only about 500 gallons of water are involved, but where there's water, there've got to be fish, right? Well, there've been a variety over the years. In the small pond I raise tropical fish six months out of the year, usually fancy guppies. In the larger pond, you might find a crappie, a bluegill, or even a smallmouth, and most of the time there will be two turtles and, as I mentioned earlier in this book, some leftover crawdads that I drop in after outings.

It didn't take Sheffield long to discover the critters. With no upland game birds to flush in the backyard, he decided the next best thing was stalking whatever was in the larger pond. If he couldn't see something clearly enough, he'd put his head beneath the surface of the water all the way up to his ears so he could get a better look. One day I decided to take a series of pictures of his stalking; I even attached a snorkel to his collar. I swear it looked just as though he were breathing through this apparatus while his head was submerged. Eventually, I'd tell him, "Find the fish, Sheffield, find the fish," and he'd run to the pond and begin looking.

One day in the early spring I was walking the shoreline at Lake

Arrowhead looking for smallmouth. I noticed Sheffield run out on a dock and then stop. He was staring into the water. Then I saw it as well—a bass. And then it dawned on me. If he could spot them at home, why not here? And that's exactly how we fish now. He's got better sight than I do. So we walk along and I just say, "Find me a fish, Sheffield, get me a fish." You ought to see his excitement when I land that bass, let him sniff it, and then release it for another day. Yes, there is something to this sight fishing after all. If you're skeptical about this, join me sometime. After all, seeing is believing.

And speaking of seeing, that is what's involved in life as well. We need to keep our eyes open or we'll not only miss out on that shoreline bass, we'll miss out on a lot of life. I've seen anglers so intent on fishing that they never notice the beauty of the foliage, trees, wildlife, or clouds. For me, the environment above the water is as important as what's underneath.

I've seen a husband so involved in what he was doing or thinking that he failed to notice his wife was wearing a new dress or had re-decorated their bedroom. That doesn't make for a pleasant evening.

What do you see around you? Is there something important to look at, but you fail to see? It happens. It's happened to me. Perhaps the intensity we give to searching and looking for fish could be directed elsewhere at times.

Jesus had something to say about seeing. In the book of Mark He said, "Having eyes, do you not see?" (8:18 NASB). In Matthew He said, "Therefore I speak to them in parables; because while seeing they do not see" (13:13 NASB). It's possible to see but not get the message. It's possible to see but not understand. That's what Jesus was concerned about here. Life is more than fishing. It's more than stalking a bass. It's about a relationship with Jesus. It's understanding who He is, and what He taught, and then seeing life through a different lens, one that really takes the glare out of life.

"I'd Rather Do It Myself"

31

Have you ever been around someone who tries to take all the credit? There are some people who always have to turn the attention around to themselves no matter what. If you've been out fishing enough you've run into them. They cleverly guide conversations to what they've done, are doing, or will do. They're also good at answering questions you haven't asked!

Then there are those who are unbelievably self-sufficient. I heard the story of two men who sat next to each other on a flight. After going on and on about his accomplishments, one of them said, "You know, I'm a self-made man." The other man, who by now was fed up with listening to all this stuff, replied, "Really? Well, that sure relieves God of that responsibility."

When I first started bass fishing I was in my fifties. I knew I had a lot to learn, and I didn't have fifty more years to learn it either. I read books and magazines and watched videos and various bass programs on The Nashville Network (TNN). I familiarized myself with the names and insights of pros such as Denny Brauer, Kevin VanDam, Hank Parker, Bill Dance, Shaw Grigsby, Jimmy Houston, and Al and Ron Lindner. I also hired different guides to teach me as much as I could learn and as quickly as I could. After meeting the guides and getting out on the water, I'd say, "I'm really a novice. I'd like to learn as much as I can from you. So whatever you can do, I'd really appreciate it." I got some silent stares. I found out later they weren't used to hearing this from clients. Too often their clients tried to impress the guides or even instruct them. That doesn't make sense. Why hire a pro if you don't want to learn? I guess some people feel like they know it all or can do it all.

I remember hearing a story about a woodpecker. It seems he went through life much like other woodpeckers. He flew from tree to tree. He drilled holes, searched for grubs, and now and then ran from a hungry cat. He was comfortable. Life was good. He knew what he was doing.

Then it happened! One day, as he was going about his business of boring into tree trunks—suddenly, unexpectedly, without announcement or warning—a bolt of lightning zapped his tree, splitting it right down the middle. The bird was thrown several feet into the air. When he landed, he was lying on his back on the forest floor. He slowly opened his eyes. He was dazed, his feathers were smoking, and his beak was singed. He got up and shook himself. As he surveyed what had happened to the giant oak, he rubbed his smoldering beak and raised an eyebrow. Then he stood straight up, thrust out his charred chest feathers, and strutted off through the woods, saying, "Man, I didn't know I had that in me!"

How many of us are like that woodpecker? We spend our days plugging along, content to walk in the familiar, well-worn ruts of life. Then suddenly God intervenes in our lives, moves us out of our rut, changes our routine, and lifts us above the forest floor for a brief moment—all by doing something that takes us totally by surprise. We look at our smoking beaks, dust ourselves off, and say, "Did I do that? I didn't know I had that in me."[27]

Perhaps we need to give credit where it's due. We also need to realize that we're not as self-sufficient as we think. Perhaps there's something different you'd like to be doing in your Christian life. If you don't know, ask God for instructions. If you do know, ask Him to take you by surprise, so you can say, "I didn't know I had that in me." Or better yet, "Thanks, Lord!"

"Call to me and I will answer you and tell you great and unsearchable things you do not know" (Jeremiah 33:3).

We don't own our bodies. They are not ours. They never were; never will be. Our bodies belong to God. We are able to present them to God as a sacrifice.

Sacrifice Your Body

32

There were three of us that morning in a rental boat. We headed out to a cove where the fish had been hitting all week. It was one of the most scenic spots on the small lake. You could hear a covey of quail calling back and forth in the brush on the gradual slope of a hillside where some cattle grazed.

We'd been there a short time when another boat appeared and anchored about 150 yards away. Now, to say the lone occupant was large is an understatement. Sitting in the stern of his 16-footer, he began to fish as well as imbibe one can of beer after another. He went through one six-pack, and then as time went on started another. Every now and then he'd stand up, which was scary, considering his condition. And when he sat down we wondered if his small boat would take it.

Well, it finally happened. And, no, not when he stood up, but while he was sitting. I don't know if he dozed off or what, but he slowly rolled off the back of the boat and, with a splash, went under. He popped up quickly, mad as a wet rooster and cussing to beat the band! We immediately started in his direction, but as soon as we saw him pull himself back into the boat, plus knowing how angry he was, we reconsidered the wisdom of helping out. He pulled that anchor up, yanked the starter on the boat, and headed out of the cove at full speed. I'm sure he couldn't see where he was going because his weight made the bow stick up so high. We looked at each other and shook our heads.

Later when we pulled up to the dock we asked one of the workers, "Did you see a big wet guy in a boat who was pretty well soused?" He said, "Oh, yeah, we could see him coming in. He never slowed down . . . just hit the dock full speed. Fortunately he hit one of the bumper tires so he didn't do much damage. He almost catapulted out of the boat, though. If he'd been normal size he would have. Fortunately, that 10-horse motor was all he had. He stomped and staggered off the dock. We stayed out of his way. Man, what a menace."

On the one hand, the drunk boater provided us a good story and a good laugh. On the other, it was kind of sad. Fishing is a great experience, but this guy messed it up. And the man on the dock was right. The guy was a menace, first, to all the other boaters on the lake. You don't drink and drive—whether on the water or in a car. The guy drove home drunk and angry—the two major causes of accidents. And, unfortunately, he was a menace to himself by drinking and driving and also by how he had let his body go.

How does *your* body look? Go ahead; if you have a full-length mirror at home, check yourself out. If not, use a mirror at the gym where you work out. (You *do* work out, don't you?) Is there the right amount of muscle tone versus body fat? Or do you get the feeling someone slipped in one of those curved mirrors found in carnival fun houses? We come in all shapes and sizes. We can do very little about our height, except to make sure that we stand up straight. Our horizontal dimensions—our width—well, that's another matter.

It's interesting to note and understand what Scripture says about our bodies: "Therefore, I urge you, brothers, in view of God's mercy, to offer your bodies as living sacrifices, holy and pleasing to God—this is your spiritual act of worship" (Romans 12:1).

When sacrificial animals were presented to God in the Old Testament, they had to be the best specimens, without blemish. If we are called to be a walking, breathing sacrifice, people should be able to look at us and say, "Now, *that's* a sacrifice to God." But will they end the statement with an exclamation point or a question mark? An exclamation point says, "You're in great shape! Wow!" A question mark says, "You're a living sacrifice? You have to be kidding!"

I remember a cartoon featuring a couple of older men obviously out of shape. One says to the other, "I'm at the place where it's difficult to refer to my body as a temple of the Lord. It's more like a rotunda!"

Some people can't do much about the shape they're in because of heredity, a glandular imbalance, disease, or a metabolism problem. But most of us can!

I'm sorry to bring it up, but do you exercise? Is it regular and aerobic? You say you don't have the money or time to go to a gym? That's all right. Plenty of used home exercise equipment is available. Or you can do the brisk walk routine, memorizing Scripture or praying along the way. Many do. And if you have a dog, take your four-legged friend along. He or she will appreciate it. If you own a cat . . . forget it. Finally, for those who think fishing is exercise, sorry, but it doesn't compute.

Remember, our bodies are temples of the Holy Spirit (see 1 Corinthians 6:19). They belong to God, who says through this Scripture: "Treat well what I've given to you, for in so doing, you honor me and you become a testimony to others about your relationship with me."

*ℒet your eyes look directly forward,
and your gaze be straight before you.
Take heed to the path of your feet,
then all your ways will be sure.*

—Proverbs 4:25–26 RSV

A One-Track Mind

33

$\mathcal{S}$everal summers ago I taught a two-week graduate-level course at a seminary. One day I gave an exam. The good part would be finding out what the students were learning. On the downside, it was going to take several hours to read and grade the exams. Stuck with that chore, I was determined to enjoy myself. This was a number of years ago—before I had discovered bass and was still into trout—so I took those exams and drove out to Lake Irvine where I proceeded to rent a boat. After grabbing my fishing gear and the exams, I found a quiet place on the lake, dropped my anchor, threw out a line, propped up the rod, spread out the papers, and began to read.

Not more than five minutes later a fish smashed into the bait. The rod started bouncing so I dropped the exams and worked to pull in the fish. Mission accomplished, I picked up the papers with my salmon-egg and fish-slimed fingers and resumed grading. Ten minutes later the same scenario played itself out again. For the next hour this was the pattern. It was hard to really focus on what I was reading since I knew I'd be disrupted in a few moments. I practically had one eye on the exams and one on the rod. And then the fish went into a biting frenzy. At that point I gave up grading and started some serious fishing. Twenty minutes later I was standing there with exams strewn all over the bottom of the boat, fish flopping on them, and the jar of salmon eggs tipped over and rolling around.

I wish you could have seen and heard the students' reactions the next day when I returned their papers. Seeing reddish stains and the imprint of a dirty boot, someone asked, "What happened to this page? It looks like someone dropped garbage on it." Good observation. Another student held his paper up to his nose and said, "Yuck! This stinks. It smells like a fish." It was great. I'd never had such responses to returned exams. At the same time, I think they were pleased with their grades. It seems I was fairly easy on them since I had made such a mess. And honestly, a few exams were pretty hard to read after the fish slime and water had made the ink run. (In case you're wondering, I waited until the end of class that day to tell them what had happened.)

I never tried that again. Working on the exams distracted me from fully enjoying fishing, and fishing distracted me from doing my best job at grading. It was as though each activity pulled me in a different direction. It would have been better to concentrate on doing one thing well at a time.

This reminds me of a recent experience. A friend and I were out fishing in a small boat on a lake where you could only use trolling motors. Mine is a Motor Guide with a 43-pound thrust. My friend had also brought his trolling motor, which only had a 15-pound thrust. Even though we knew they wouldn't balance each other out, we decided to put both motors on the back to generate more speed. This isn't unusual. I've seen four on the back of one boat, and I've even seen one used on a float tube.

We started off and cranked up both motors to full speed. After a while I said, "Don, you know, I thought we'd be going faster. I really don't see much difference in having two motors." I played with the speed of both, but it stayed the same. With the 15-amp sounding more like a threshing machine, I began to look at it a bit more carefully. Then I asked that fateful (and dumb) question, "Don, does your motor have a reverse switch on it?" I got a stare that expressed something like, *Well, of course it does . . . Why are you asking?* That was it. I knew our problem. You can't make much headway when one motor is pushing you forward and the other backward. Of course, you've got to get them in sync to really get anywhere.

I guess a lot of people have that problem in life. Part of them is drawn one way, and part another way. It's hard to move forward when something is causing you to regress. And sometimes we simply don't make the progress we want because our attention is divided between two things (such as fishing and grading exams).

Perhaps when Paul wrote the following words, they were given to help us stay focused and to make sure all of our energy is pulling together. This is especially true in living a Christian life. It's easy to get distracted and diverted from what God wants us to do and become.

> But one thing I do: forgetting what lies behind and reaching forward to what lies ahead, I press on toward the goal for the prize of the upward call of God in Christ Jesus. (Philippians 3:13–14 NASB)

*W*hat is impossible with men is
possible with God.

—*Luke 18:27*

Mission Possible

34

$\mathcal{M}$ost anglers are optimistic. If they see water they believe there's got to be a fish there. I've never gone fishing with anyone (yet) who says, "Well, we'll go out, but nothing we do is going to work. It's just impossible to catch any bass around here. I don't care what you use, it won't work." Frankly, I'd rather go out with someone who brings their tackle store along with them and says, "Something is going to work today. It may take time, but we'll find something they'll hit on." I'll go out with those anglers.

Still, some people live their lives based on phrases like: Can't be done. Tried it. Nope, it's impossible. Words like these bring progress to a roaring halt. I don't like to hear them. It's true that experience can sometimes cause us to make statements that stifle the learning experiences of life. Some people seem to have the gift of throwing in the towel; they feel it's a waste of time to try something new. But what would happen if we eliminated words from our vocabularies that breed impossibility? What if we replaced these words with "Let's give it a try"?

A few years ago Pastor Lloyd Ogilvie wrote a book with the title *Lord of the Impossible.* I imagine all of us have faced obstacles that we thought were impossible. But the question is, do we believe Jesus is Lord of *those* circumstances?

I read a story in *Bassmaster* magazine about a young man by the name of Clay Dyer. He fished in local club tournaments and B.A.S.S. Federation events. Clay was born without legs and a left arm, and only had the upper part of his right arm. But he's not limited. He can tie on baits. He can tell you the taste of various plastic worms since he rigs them with his lips and tongue. He's accurate in his casting and has learned to use his whole body. He can whip a plug out there over thirty yards. He can play as well as land his own fish, take out the hook, and release the fish. He doesn't have any special tackle. He uses a long-handle bait casting outfit. All without any artificial limbs. Who runs his boat for him? He does. Clay also runs his trolling motor. Here is a young man who doesn't have the word *impossible* in his vocabulary. But he does have optimism and perseverance![28]

Early in the twentieth century someone had the bright idea of creating a parachute. Wouldn't you have loved to have been there when the inventor tried to explain his idea for the first time? Can you imagine the facial expressions and comments of the people around him? I bet he had a time getting any volunteers to try it. Fortunately, the inventor was deaf to the word *impossible.* He tried, and yes, there were failures, but he kept at it. He persisted. Over the years parachutes have saved countless lives.

You may have a limited perception of what God can do in your life. Perhaps it's because family members or people at work or church keep telling you, "It's impossible!" But are they really experts? If you wonder about God's power, it may help to read the following passage aloud each day for a week:

> "The person who trusts me will not only do what I'm doing, but even greater things, because I, on my way to the Father, am giving you the same work to do that I've been doing. You can count on it. From now on, whatever you request along the lines of who I am and what I am doing, I'll do it" (John 14:12–14 The Message).

Have you ever heard the phrase, "The impossible is the untried"? Much of what we experience today in our homes or on the road wouldn't be there if inventors had listened to people who said, "Impossible!" This is not a word God ever uses to describe our circumstances, so why should we? Instead, He says the opposite: "Try it. Go for it. Let's do it together."[29]

Worse than being lost is the failure to admit you're lost.

Fighting a Lost Cause

35

*L*ost?

"Me? Naw, I'm just taking a new way to get there."

Very few guys will admit to being lost. But it happens. Women, on the other hand, are more likely to stop and ask for directions. It's true. Just mention this to a group of couples and note the reaction you get. But you'd have to agree that it is more difficult to stop and ask for directions today. Gas stations used to be called "service stations." Today that's a joke. You're lucky to find a living soul at a gas station, and if you do, their awareness of directions and locations is practically nonexistent.

Know what's worse than being lost in a car? Being lost in your boat. Whenever you go out on a large lake or a new river system, you've got to remember your bearings and set some markers, otherwise you could spend all night lost. This is especially a problem on some of the lakes in Canada where the shoreline is nothing but a constant tree line and there's only one small isolated cabin that's partially hidden in the woods. That's why a GPS or compass is so helpful.

We could have used a compass the day we took our boat out to the breakwater off of Long Beach, California, about twenty years ago. It was a beautiful, clear, sunny day that morning—on shore. We cruised out the channel and headed toward the breakwater, hoping for some great bass fishing. Suddenly the fog descended. No problem. All we had to do was keep going the same direction and we'd come to the breakwater less than a mile away. So we kept going and going and going. After a while, my fishing partner and I looked at each other, wondering, *Where'd they move that breakwater? We should have been there by now.* Yes, a typical male response—someone had *moved* the breakwater! Not that we could have been lost, right? Anyway, we started cutting a large circle trying to find the breakwater. Fifteen minutes later we saw a shape in the mist. "There it is . . . I think. Hey, it's rocks all right. But it looks different." It was. We had come to one of the large oil islands in the harbor. A man was walking on the top, so we asked him where we were.

"You guys lost, huh?"

My partner and I looked at each other until I finally said, "I guess so. I think we went the wrong way."

"It's easy to do," the man said. "The breakwater is two miles that way. Just use your compass. You *do* have a compass, don't you?" (Silence.) He grinned and added, "Well, good luck anyway."

We found the breakwater. And on the way home I bought a compass.

Almost everyone is guilty of repeating the same mistakes, not wanting to admit they're lost. We blindly run around in the same circle, never getting anywhere, like the characters in J. R. R. Tolkien's

The Hobbit. In this fantasy story, a band of dwarves and one little hobbit are wandering around lost in a dismal forest. Other creatures had warned them about this place, but they were hungry and decided to wander around. Now they were lost and in deep danger. They were thirsty and hungry, and all around were huge deadly spiders. They couldn't find their way out because of the height and density of the forest. They couldn't see through the foliage.

So the dwarves sent Bilbo, the hobbit, up an old tree to see if he could discover where they were and find a way out. He climbed and climbed, and as he got higher the branches got smaller and smaller. Soon he was at the top and finally able to thrust his head above the last leaves. He was startled by the dazzling sunlight and the clear sky. The rotting smell of the damp forest was gone and he could breathe fresh air. He could see!

We can see, too, if we stick our heads above the jungle and catch a vision of what God wants us to become. God's Word can give direction: "If any of you lacks wisdom, he should ask God, who gives generously to all without finding fault, and it will be given to him" (James 1:5). You won't get lost with Him.

*Reading, studying, and memorizing
God's Word will change any man.*

Saturated With the Word

36

$\mathcal{R}$ainstorms vary. Some are like a persistent mosquito just buzzing around but never going away. Some never amount to much, but you spend your day slipping your rain gear on and off again. Other storms are intense. They soak. They drench. They saturate you. The water oozes through every possible opening. Your clothes get wet and soon your skin is moist. There isn't a dry inch on your entire body. This is total saturation.

Saturation is a positive thing when it comes to the Word of God. To live a Christian life in today's world you've got to saturate yourself with God's Word.

In war, saturation bombing is often used to totally obliterate enemy positions in certain areas. Planes continuously drop load after load of bombs in a crisscross pattern until every inch of land has been covered. Similarly, as a follower of Christ, you need to allow the Holy

Spirit to saturate every inch of your heart and mind with the truth of who you are and what you are becoming in Christ.

Years ago I was fishing on a lake with one of my dogs, a sheltie. He was perched on the bow of the boat, enjoying the ride with his nose in the wind as I headed into a cove at full speed. Suddenly I changed my mind about fishing there, so I swung the boat around and reversed my direction. My dog lost his balance and went flying into the lake. I don't know who was more surprised—he or I!

I swung the boat around to where he was swimming (he wasn't too happy with me at that moment) and cut the motor. I picked him out of the water but didn't lift him into the boat right away because he was totally soaked. I held him away from the boat, gently squeezed his coat to eliminate most of the water, and only then brought him into the boat safe and sound.

My new dog is quite different from the sheltie. For one thing, he's three times heavier. As a golden retriever, he loves playing in the water. And he doesn't get soaked. His coat actually repels water. When he emerges from the water he appears wet but the water doesn't penetrate his thick coat. Within a short time, it looks as though he never went swimming.

Some of us are thick-coated like my retriever. God's truth has never thoroughly penetrated our outer layer or deeply influenced us. We haven't been fully soaked. But for growth to occur, we must saturate ourselves in God's truth.

When I was a teenager I spent a lot of time memorizing Scripture. It helped more times than I can remember. On several occasions, facing a temptation and struggling with a decision, Scripture came into my mind at the right moment. Usually it was 1 Corinthians 10:13:

But remember this—the wrong desires that come into your

life aren't anything new and different. Many others have faced exactly the same problems before you. And no temptation is irresistible. You can trust God to keep the temptation from becoming so strong that you can't stand up against it, for he has promised this and will do what he says. He will show you how to escape temptation's power so that you can bear up patiently against it. (TLB)

That message was a lifesaver for me as a young man. Unfortunately, throughout the decades of adulthood I did not make a consistent attempt to memorize God's Word. In 1995, however, a friend at a family camp, Rick Hicks, shared a section from his new book *Seeking Solid Ground*, which is about Psalm 15. He gently challenged us to memorize this psalm. It explains how to get the most out of life and be close to God.

I don't know why, but I accepted the challenge. Memorization takes a bit more work these days, but spending just two or three minutes each morning, the passage soon became mine. Now when I wake up at night I often quote Psalm 15 silently. I quote it when I'm driving. The words are reassuring. They keep me alert, on track for God. I've worked on many other passages since then. I don't want to stop.

Go ahead, let God's Word shape your life. You'll never regret it. And the more you do, the more you'll want to.

> Oh, how I love them [God's commandments]. I think about them all day long. They make me wiser than my enemies because they are my constant guide. Yes, wiser than my teachers, for I am ever thinking of your rules. They make me even wiser than the aged. (Psalm 119:97–100 TLB)[30]

*I do not have fellowship with tricky,
two-faced men; they are false
and hypocritical.*

—Psalm 26:4 TLB

Are You for "Reel"?

37

For years we've heard the advertisement for Coke: "It's the real thing." What they're saying is that it's authentic. What you see is what you get.

Some anglers are true fishermen. Others look like they are, but they're more spectator than participant. How do you spot them? It's not too hard. It could happen like this:

You're at the launch ramp getting your boat on the water. You're carefully backing down and stopping at a point where your boat will float off easily and still not sink your truck or car. You tie up your boat at the dock, park your vehicle, and walk back. That's when you see *him*. In fact, you couldn't miss him. He's got a big truck and a 22-foot boat. The problem is he's backing the boat down the ramp at an angle that promises doom and gloom. Other guys are pulling off the ramp so they don't get whacked. Finally after several tries his boat is launched, but instead of taking off to fish, he notices you standing there at your boat and heads over. You're stuck. You can't untie your boat in time to escape. You know what's coming. The guy starts in.

"Hey there, fisherman. I see you're going to head out in that big lake in that little ol' boat of yours. You sure it's big enough?" As you open your mouth to answer he keeps on talking. "Now, you take my boat. It's a real boat for a real bass fisherman. It's the latest. I just got me this new Nitro 911 CDC, and it hauls with this 225 FEI Merc. I even got three separate wells for when I start my tournament tour. It's got the newest Zercom LCD flashers with all them pixel matrix stuff. Then look at these here poles I got to fish with." (Under your breath you mutter, "Rod, it's a rod.") "I got this seven-foot all-star T40X graphite with 70 million moderlus and SIC guides. Oh, this baby will bring in all those hawgs." (Now you're beginning to groan and fight the urge to shake your head. Your friend, who is watching you from behind this guy, is grinning from ear to ear knowing what's going on inside of you.) "I slapped a new Daiwa autocast anti-reverse reel with six ball bearings on it. No more bird's nest for me. I'll whip that lure out there and nail those bass. I put 20-pound test SpiderWire on it, too."

Right then and there you see your chance. You interrupt and say, "That's great line, isn't it? The only problem I have is biting off the slack after I tie a Palomar knot. You have that problem, too?"

"Me, ah, well, not really. I bite right through it. It's no big deal."

Everyone on the dock who heard your question and his answer bursts out laughing. They know all about SpiderWire. The guy realizes that something's wrong and says, "Well, guys, see ya. Gotta go get a 10-pounder." He heads off to another dock where there's an unsuspecting angler loading his boat, and you hear him say, "Hey, there, fisherman . . ." and it begins all over again. When you come back hours later he's still there talking to whomever he can trap. He never left. He never fished. He had all the equipment, all the lingo, but he wasn't the real thing. He wasn't a real angler. Looking the part doesn't make you a bass angler. You have to practice, learn, grow, and fish.

Some people who call themselves Christians are like this. They look the part and talk the language, but something's missing. When Jesus really comes into our life something happens. We're different. We change. And we do this to such an extent that it's noticed by others. We think, speak, and act differently than others in our culture. We love Jesus and we're willing to not only tell others, but to let His love come out in the way we relate to others.

Ken Gire is one of my favorite authors. This is how he describes what our life should be like:

> So it's the end of the day, and each of us is lying on our bed, reflecting. Have I loved well? Has love been the beating heart pulsing through all my activities? Can it be heard in all my conversations? Seen in my eyes? Felt when other people are in my presence? Was the truth I spoke today spoken in love? Were the decisions I made today based on love? Were my reactions? My devotions?
>
> Have I loved well?
>
> If we answer yes to that question, it is enough. It may not be enough for our employer. It may not be enough for our fellow workers. It may not be enough for all the carpools and committees and other things on our calendar. It may not even be enough for us. But it is enough for God. And that should make it enough for us.[31]

Whoever trusts in his riches will fall, but the righteous will thrive like a green leaf.

—Proverbs 11:28

The More the Better?

38

We're encouraged to accumulate. The more the better. The bigger the better. Or at least that's what the ads tell us. Possess as much as you can and keep trading up.

Now, I have to admit that some of us bass anglers do have quite a bit of equipment. But I don't think it's accumulating for the sake of accumulation. One rod in the boat just isn't enough. Nor are two or three or even four. When I first got into bass fishing, I'd see guys carrying eight rods to their boat and wondered why. After a few months I learned that you need different lengths for different purposes. You need a rod for flippin'. You need a good crankin' rod. The action varies, so you need several rods for different lure weights. Not only that, if you're using a topwater lure and that bass misses it, you may want to come back immediately with another presentation, this time using a plastic worm to fool him. But you don't want to take the time to switch baits! You set one rod down and pick up the other. In the case of fishing rods, more is better. They serve a purpose. They're functional.

Some people accumulate just to have more—be it status, wealth, or bragging rights. Jesus said something about this:

> And someone in the crowd said to Him, "Teacher, tell my brother to divide the family inheritance with me." But He said to him, "Man, who appointed Me a judge or arbiter over you?" And He said to them, "Beware, and be on your guard against every form of greed; for not even when one has an abundance does his life consist of his possessions." And He told them a parable, saying, "The land of a certain rich man was very productive. And he began reasoning to himself, saying, 'What shall I do, since I have no place to store my crops?' And he said, 'This is what I will do: I will tear down my barns and build larger ones, and there I will store all my grain and my goods. And I will say to my soul, "Soul, you have many goods laid up for many years to come; take your ease, eat, drink and be merry."' But God said to him, 'You fool! This very night your soul is required of you; and now who will own what you have prepared?' So is the man who lays up treasure for himself, and is not rich toward God" (Luke 12:13–21 NASB).

Noted preacher and writer George Buttrick, in *The Parables of Jesus*, said this about material possessions:

> A man must keep things at their distance. He must be *in* the material world, but not *of* it. He must say to his possessions: "You are not my life. You never can be my life. There is a gulf set between you and me." The gulf is proved because his possessions cannot even answer him! But the Rich Man thought so persist-

ently and with such concentration about his "goods" that the necessary line of distinction between *him* and *his* was erased. His life was lost in his livelihood. . . . He had no thought for God. "*My* fruits," he called them; "*my* grain." But in what sense were they his? Could he command the sap in the tree, the fertility in the soil? Were sunrise and sunset under his control? Was the Faithfulness of returning seasons his merit? If the rain had been withheld, where then would have been his wealth: "The *ground* brought forth plentifully"; all the man could do was to take nature's tides at the flood. He was carried to fortune on a fecundity, a light, a heat, a constancy in nature's cycles, which are boundless mysteries of blessing—and he called them "mine"! His title was earned—"Thou fool!"

Can you relate to the following prayer? I can.

Dear God,
  I so much want to be in control.
  I want to be the master of my own destiny.
  Still I know you are saying:
  "Let me take you by the hand and lead you. Accept my love and trust that where I will bring you, the deepest desires of your heart will be fulfilled."
  Lord, open my hands to receive your gift of love. Amen.
(Henri Nouwen, *With Open Hands*)[32]

*He who endures to the end
will be saved.*

—Matthew 10:22 RSV

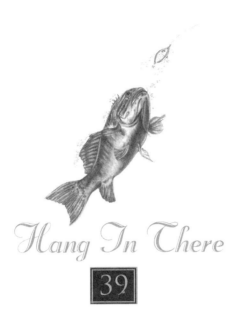

Hang In There

39

𝒥 read the story of a teenager fishing one of the San Diego lakes in a float tube. As he was cruising along the shoreline he spotted a huge bass—the biggest he had ever seen—protecting its bed. He began casting a plastic worm to the bass. He barely twitched it in front, trying to entice that fish. Again and again he cast. He kept presenting that bait, but the bass kept ignoring it. A half hour went by, then an hour. Some anglers would stop to watch for a while but then move on, making comments like, "Give it up, kid. That bass will never bite." However, a few others encouraged him: "Hey—hang in there. You never know." Two hours went by. Finally the bass's patience with this irritating kid and his plastic worm ran out. The bass struck. So did the young man. And several minutes later he held that fish up, weighed it, took a quick picture, and released it—all 14 pounds of it! Yeah, it was worth hanging in there.

The expression "Hang in there" was taken to heart by Henry Dempsey. He was piloting a flight between two small towns on the East Coast when he heard a strange noise coming from the rear of the plane. He handed the controls over to his copilot and went back to check out the noise. To his surprise, he found that the rear door had not been secured before takeoff. Just then the plane hit some turbulence and slammed Henry against the door. It flew open, sucking Henry out over the cold ocean thousands of feet below.

The copilot noticed two things: the open-door warning light and the fact that Henry had disappeared. Realizing what must have happened, he radioed for a helicopter search over that section of the ocean.

The plane landed, and Henry was found. But not where they thought he would be. As Henry was being sucked out the door, he had grabbed the outside ladder and hung on for dear life, even while the plane descended several thousand feet at 200 miles per hour. During the landing he kept his head raised just twelve inches off the ground, giving him an upclose view of the runway. When he was discovered, they had to pry his fingers away from the ladder. This guy *really* hung in there.

Sometimes it's difficult to hang in there—to persevere—especially when we hit turbulence in our lives. We'd rather bail out instead of working it out. When there's difficulty at work, we head for the want ads. When our kids don't take care of their responsibilities, we'd like to ship them out. When we're at odds with our spouse, we may even think a change would be nice.

Sure, life is unfair. Some people are difficult to get along with. But hanging in there and resolving problems may be a better solution than bailing out. God's Word talks to us time and time again about patience, endurance, and sticking it out:

Therefore, since we have so great a cloud of witnesses surrounding us, let us also lay aside every encumbrance, and the sin which so easily entangles us, and let us run with endurance the race that is set before us, fixing our eyes on Jesus, the author and perfecter of faith, who for the joy set before Him endured the cross, despising the shame, and has sat down at the right hand of the throne of God. For consider Him who has endured such hostility by sinners against Himself, so that you may not grow weary and lose heart. (Hebrews 12:1–3 NASB)

Patience literally means "long suffering." In other words, being able to continue to hang in there and not throw in the towel.

Some say that they can't endure. It's too difficult by themselves. They're right. That's why patience is part of the fruit of the Spirit (see Galatians 5:22–23). It takes God's power to help you hang in there. You're running a lifelong race, but fortunately you are not on your own. He is with you.

When you're struggling, turn back to the psalmist: "I waited patiently for the Lord; And He inclined to me, and heard my cry" (Psalm 40:1 NASB).[33]

*Therefore be careful how you walk,
not as unwise men, but as wise.*

—Ephesians 5:15 NASB

Not Too Swift!

40

Sometimes people do things in life that are, well, what others would describe as "not too swift." (Really a polite way of saying "that was downright dumb.") I know I've been guilty of this. Often it's because we're just not being careful. For instance, we're rushing and fail to read the directions, or we ignore advice we know is true. Whatever the reason, the results can be humorous or sometimes disastrous.

One day I was fishing at a small lake with a friend. This was during the "BB" time in my life—"before I owned a boat"—so we had rented a 16-foot aluminum. After fishing for a while, a rainstorm hit. Now, I don't mind rain. I've fished in rain, sleet, and snow. But this one was a drencher and it didn't want to quit. So after an hour of getting soaked with no fish to show for our effort, we decided to head for shore, take a break, and wait it out. I don't like to stop fishing, but it seemed the best thing to do, especially after seeing everyone else on the lake do the same.

About two hours later the rain stopped, and we ambled back to the dock and found the boat loaded with water. I suggested to my fishing partner that he bring out all of our gear while I bailed out the boat. He left and I started, coffee can in hand. Man, there was a lot of water. Several minutes later I looked up to see my partner approaching and a couple of other guys standing by and smiling. As I was finishing the job, my partner said, "Norm, you're really doing a good job bailing out that boat. There's only one problem. That's not our boat. But I bet these guys here appreciate your help!" My hand stopped in midair just as I was dumping another can over the side. I glanced up, surrounded by smiles, then looked at the number on the boat. "Oh, no! After all that work!" When I looked up again, they weren't smiling. This time they were rolling with laughter. I joined in, knowing it would be *the* story on the dock that day.

That day, my oversight led to a good laugh and a great memory. But it doesn't always turn out that way. Sometimes not being careful can have disastrous results.

When we don't listen carefully we can misinterpret words and end up hurting a friend or family member.

When we believe everything in the news without checking the sources we may act on misinformation.

When someone spreads gossips and we believe it without checking it out we could be participating in slander. We are also failing to exhibit love that "is ever ready to believe the best of every person" (1 Corinthians 13:7 AMP).

When we're too busy with work, hobbies (fishing?), TV, or even our family to spend a few minutes a day in prayer and reading Scripture we can slowly begin to drift. God wants us to be careful, especially in our relationship with Him.

It's Your Choice—
Change or . . .

41

I hope the way I'm fishing for bass is changing. I hope it's different than a year ago and for the better. There's a lot to learn. But at times I'm shocked at the number of anglers who stay in their comfort zone year after year. They fish the same way, in the same places, and with the same lures as they did ten years ago. It's safe. It eliminates the risk of failing. It also eliminates the potential for greater success.

I used to go to the same spots year after year. Why? I knew I could catch fish there. Sure, heading to those spots I would notice others that looked inviting, but I didn't want to miss the good old reliable places. One year I decided to change my strategy; I'd fish some of the old places but add new ones. And sure enough, some of the new locations did work out better.

It's all right to change. Life is full of change. But many people don't want to. The word *change* means to make different; to give a different course or direction; to replace one thing with another; to make a shift from one to another; to undergo transformation, transition, or substitution. However, many people see change as negative, something that implies inferiority, inadequacy, and failure. No wonder so many people resist the idea of change. Who wants to feel inferior and inadequate?

People are a lot like trees; they either grow or they die. There's no standing still. A tree dies when its roots become blocked. God has made us in such a way that when we choose to allow the circumstances of our lives to keep us from growing, we become mentally, spiritually, and, eventually, physically dead. Pastors, physicians, and psychologists spend their lives trying to help individuals (even institutions) who have stopped growing because of their choices.[34]

What's the opposite of growing? Consider these words:

stagnant	stale	sluggish	lethargic
passive	lazy	dormant	dead
lifeless	deteriorated	degenerate	in a decline
gone to seed	vegetative	atrophied	decayed

What's your first thought after scanning this list? Mine was "Yuck!" I don't think anyone would want to be described as lethargic, stagnant, deteriorated, or atrophied. Yet that's what we choose when we choose not to grow.

Tim Hansel tells a great story about what it's like to be around people who have chosen to play it safe, to stay stuck, to not grow:

A close friend of mine was asked back to his forty-year high school reunion. For months he saved to take his wife back to the place and the people he'd left four decades before. The closer the time came for the reunion, the more excited he became, thinking of all the wonderful stories he would hear about the changes and the accomplishments these old friends would tell him. One night before he left he even pulled out his old yearbooks and read the silly statements and the good wishes for the future that students write to each other. He wondered if any others had encountered this Christ who had changed him so profoundly. He even tried to guess what some of his friends would look like, and what kind of jobs and families some of these special friends had.

The day came to leave and I drove them to the airport. Their energy was almost contagious. "I'll pick you up on Sunday evening, and you can tell me all about it," I said. "Have a great time."

Sunday evening arrived. As I watched them get off the plane, my friend seemed almost despondent. I almost didn't want to ask, but finally I said, "Well, how was the reunion?"

"Tim," the man said, "it was one of the saddest experiences of my life."

"Good grief," I said, more than a little surprised. "What happened?"

"It wasn't what happened but what didn't happen. It has been forty years, forty years—and they haven't changed. They had simply gained weight, changed clothes, gotten jobs ... but they hadn't really changed. And what I experienced was maybe one of the most tragic things I could ever imagine about life. For reasons I can't fully understand, it seems as though some people choose not to change."

There was a long silence as we walked back to the car. On the drive home, he turned to me and said, "I never, never want that to be said of me, Tim. Life is too precious, too sacred, too important. If you ever see me go stagnant like that, I hope you give me a quick, swift kick where I need it—for Christ's sake. I hope you'll love me enough to challenge me to keep growing."[35]

Let's face it. When you boil the Christian life down to the basics, the name of the game is change. Those who want to learn—who are willing to look at themselves in the mirror before grabbing the binoculars to view and judge others, who refuse to stay in a rut, who make time to listen for the still, small voice of the Holy Spirit—these are the ones God is free to use, to bless, to honor. These people know what it means to be "more than conquerors" (Romans 8:37).

Change *is* possible for those of us who are believers in Christ Jesus, because our faith is an inward transformation, not just an outward conformity. When Paul says, "My little children, for whom I labor in birth again until *Christ is formed in you*" (Galatians 4:19 NKJV, italics added), he is telling us that we have to embrace change and let Jesus live *in* and *through* us.

When a hawk is attacked by crows, the hawk doesn't counterattack. He just soars higher and higher until the crows tire and leave him alone.

Critiquing Criticism

42

$\mathcal{D}$o you enjoy criticism? Probably not. Does it make you feel better? Probably not. Do you usually say, "You're right. Thanks for telling me"? Probably not. Then why, when we need all the help we can get, do most of us resist criticism?

Our response to criticism often depends on who is giving it and why. When it's unsolicited or from a perfect stranger, it often feels like a put-down. At the same time, criticism from someone we love or admire isn't always welcome, either. I've seen kids so discouraged from their dad's criticism about the way they tied on the lure, cast, tried to set the hook, played the fish, held the rod—you name it— that they never wanted to fish again. That should never happen. I've sometimes felt the same way after being with a seasoned angler who hands out "advice" packaged like destructive criticism. I end up feeling terrible and determined not to follow their advice even if it is good.

Criticism in the form of advice or encouragement is a lot easier to handle. You don't feel criticized; you want to hear what the person has to say.

The Bible, too, has something to say about this. It uses the word *reproof,* which means "to correct or to convince." Sometimes God uses His Word to correct or convince us; other times He uses people. The point is, we *are* going to face criticism and correction in life. So, what's the best way to handle it? First, we need to understand the difference between constructive and destructive criticism. To do this you've got to ask:

Is the purpose of the statement being made to me positive in intent—does it build me up? Or is it intended to be negative—to tear me down and hurt me? Look beyond the words that you hear. Pick up the attitude of what is being said. There's a big difference between a kind, gentle attitude and one that's judgmental.

Also, *when is the correction given?* If it's done publicly, the other person is off base. Is it given for your personal benefit, or does it come from the other person's personal hurt?

Second, *look beyond the criticism and consider who said it.* That may help you decide whether you should accept it or ignore it. Do you respect this person's insights and opinions? Does this person have a pattern of criticism?

Third, *watch your own attitude toward the critic.* Make sure you don't react and retaliate with criticism. When you do, you allow this person to control you and shape you into his or her own image! You eventually become just like the person you don't want to be!

A healthier way to respond can be found in God's Word:

This is the kind of life you've been invited into, the kind of life Christ lived. He suffered everything that came His way so you would know that it could be done, and also know how to do it, step-by-step.

"He never did one thing wrong.

Not once said anything amiss."

They called him every name in the book and He said nothing back. He suffered in silence, content to let God set things right. (1 Peter 2:21–23 THE MESSAGE)

Fourth, *keep in mind that everyone will be criticized.* You may be criticized because you are a Christian. That's good. It affirms the fact that you are living your life contrary to society's standards. That's what you want, even when you're out there fishing. You're called to do this. Remember that Jesus was criticized. He was called a glutton (see Matthew 11:19); a drunkard (see Luke 7:34); a Samaritan (see John 8:48); and a friend of sinners (see Matthew 11:19; Mark 2:16).

Fifth, *don't start or join a crusade to stick around critical people trying to prove they're wrong.* It could be a waste of energy. The world is filled with plenty of positive, encouraging people—spend your time with them. It will help keep you from being critical. The key: don't battle critical people, rise above them.[36]

He who overcomes will, like them, be dressed in white. I will never blot out his name from the book of life, but will acknowledge his name before my Father and his angels.

—Revelation 3:5

One for the Record Book

43

These aren't fish stories. They're really true. Still, you might have difficulty believing them.

In 1993 a man and his eight-year-old son went bass fishing at Lake Casitas near Ojai, California. The lake is home to some large bass (the record is a 21-pound, 3-ounce bass caught in 1980), so this dad, who had caught numerous 8- and 9-pounders but nothing larger, was hoping to break the 10-pound barrier. They put their boat in the lake and went to one of their favorite spots. About an hour later he was doing a slow retrieve when he got slammed. The fish jumped and he missed setting the hook. The plug fell to the water and skidded across. But before he could tighten the line the bass hit again. Thinking he had missed once again, he set the hook a third time and finally felt the weight of the bass. As he continued to play his fish, it seemed like a lot of deadweight more than anything else. It wasn't until he got the bass close to the boat that he realized what was going on. Two large bass were hooked to the plug—one on the front treble hook and one on the back. They were swimming in tandem.

After playing the fish a bit more, the man brought them to the side where his young son waited with the net. He couldn't lift the net so his dad helped out. You can imagine their excitement, especially after weighing the fish: one registered an even 12 pounds and the other 11 pounds, 12 ounces. Can you believe it? I can. I've seen the picture. What an impressive record.[37]

Another fish story features a fellow named Dave Romeo, who wanted to get into the *Guinness Book of Records* for catching the most bass in a season. He read all the books on bass fishing and studied bass habits for three years, keeping a detailed record of every bass he caught. And I mean detailed. He tracked dates, times, locations, baits, lures, and weather patterns. In 1984 he started his attempt at the record in New York. When he wasn't working, Dave fished fourteen hours a day, averaging close to forty bass each day over a period of seventy-seven days. His final record-breaking count? Three thousand and one fish, and all but twenty-eight were released. He caught several fish more than once, including one bass at least six times, and he ended up writing a book, *Better Bass Fishing: The Dave Romeo Way*. To top it off, he met his future wife that season. She had the perfect name—well, sort of. Can you believe . . . Kim *Trout?!*[38]

Most of us wouldn't mind establishing some kind of fishing record, whether it's for the largest bass or the most caught in a single day. One summer day in 1998 I was fishing at Oso Reservoir in Southern California. For a while I watched two men in a top-notch bass boat catch one bass after another. I talked with them later and learned that they were field testers for new Shimano rods and reels.

They were really excited that day. They had caught 207 bass—their personal record.

Is your name in any record book? As great as that would be, records are made to be broken. Roger Maris broke Babe Ruth's long-standing home-run record, but not long ago Sammy Sosa and Mark McGwire topped Maris's record—twice each. It's all right to want your name in a record book. For some, it's a lifelong quest. And though they may get in, their record—and their name—could be erased anytime.

There's another book that we can have our name in, and we don't have to compete to get it there, either. It's called the Lamb's Book of Life. And once your name appears there, it will never be deleted. Is yours there? If so, rejoice. If not, it can be. Jesus said, "For God so loved the world that he gave his one and only Son, that whoever believes in him shall not perish but have eternal life" (John 3:16).

Lord, lead me as you promised me you would; otherwise my enemies will conquer me. Tell me clearly what to do, which way to turn.

—*Psalm 5:8* TLB

Setting Your Course

44

It's interesting to listen to the conversations of bass anglers. Most talk fairly openly, even dreaming aloud and making statements like, "Yeah, when I retire I'm going to get on that B.A.S.S. pro circuit. That's where the real money is. You win a few and you get all those sponsors begging you to use their stuff." Or, "I can't wait to upgrade this boat. I've had it three years now and I've just outgrown it. It's only 20-feet long and 84-inches wide. Besides, what I want is the classiest model around." Then, there are the guys who say, "I can't wait to get past that 10-pound mark with a bass. Once you get there, you're on your way. You've made your statement!"

All these statements seem to reflect the fact that most people want to accumulate, accomplish, and achieve. Don't you? We all do. We certainly wouldn't be content with the opposite of these three words, would we?

Most of us are pursuing the three A's through our jobs and the amount of money we earn. That's why many men and women put in sixty to seventy hours per week. And why not? Especially when they receive overtime pay. But *living* to accumulate, accomplish, and achieve can become an unhealthy way of life. Unfortunately, I've seen this pattern emerge in the way some people approach fishing. They seem to have lost the fun and joy of the sport. The intensity of pursuing the three A's seems to take over.

If you tend to be driven by the three A's in any area of your life, let me ask you a few questions: How long will you be able to continue your current pace? Five, ten, maybe twenty years? If you are married or get married down the road, how does this pattern fit into a healthy marriage? Will it produce children who feel valued and loved? Will it produce the lifetime of memories you want to fill the scrapbooks of your mind during your retirement years?

The effects of overwork are addressed in Scripture:

> I hated all the things I had toiled for under the sun, because I must leave them to the one who comes after me. And who knows whether he will be a wise man or a fool? Yet he will have control over all the work into which I have poured my effort and skill under the sun. (Ecclesiastes 2:18–19)

The writer of Ecclesiastes seems to be applauding himself one minute and the next he's in despair and regretting all that he has done. Talk about extremes! He's looking back after a life of effort and achievement, expressing his emptiness. "It wasn't worth it," he says. What a feeling of futility!

Have you ever had similar thoughts? Hopefully not. But lest we too experience thoughts like these, take a moment to look at your priorities and use of time. It's never too late to make a course

correction. As Dr. James Dobson says,

> I have concluded that the accumulation of wealth, even if I could achieve it, is an insufficient reason for living. When I reach the end of my days, a moment or two from now, I must look backward on something more meaningful than the pursuit of houses and land and machines and stocks and bonds. Nor is fame of any lasting benefit. I will consider my earthly existence to have been wasted unless I can recall a loving family, a consistent investment in the lives of people, and an earnest attempt to serve the God who made me. Nothing else makes much sense.[39]

So, where do you go from here? Well, you could start by evaluating how you spend your time. Look down the road a bit—to the end of your life. What do you want to be able to say about your life? How do you want to feel about your life? You can determine that by what you do now. Prepare a plan of action to live the meaningful life you want. It's not too late.

$\mathcal{G}$od makes a way when there is no
way; and when you feel like you just
can't take one more step,
He will carry you.

Can You Fish Your Worries Away?

45

I saw a man in a float tube fishing near the shore. It seemed like every third or fourth cast with his spinner bait produced a hit. I thought he was having a great time, but he sure didn't look happy. Eventually we began to talk and I found out that several things in his life were weighing him down, and he thought he'd fish to escape his worries. It wasn't working, though. That's what worry does. It snags our minds in such a way that it goes wherever we go.

What worry does is described vividly in several passages of Scripture:

> I heard and my [whole inner self] trembled; my lips quivered at the sound. Rottenness enters into my bones and under me—down to my feet—I tremble. (Habakkuk 3:16 AMP)

Anxiety in a man's heart weighs it down. (Proverbs 12:25 AMP)

A tranquil mind gives life to the flesh. (Proverbs 14:30 RSV)

All the days of the desponding and afflicted are made evil [by anxious thoughts and foreboding], but he who has a glad heart has a continual feast [regardless of circumstances]. (Proverbs 15:15 AMP)

We're told in Psalm 37 to "fret not." The dictionary defines *fret* as "to eat away, gnaw, gall, vex, worry, agitate, wear away." Worry can make you feel like you can't see the forest for the trees. It can feel like you are being eaten alive.

The effects of worry are best illustrated by a familiar scene at the Snake River in Grand Teton National Park in Wyoming. Colonies of beavers live along the riverbanks, and you often see trees at various stages of being gnawed to the ground. Some trees have slight rings around their trunks because the busy little animals have just begun to chew. Some display bare spots where several inches of bark have been eaten away. Other trees have fallen to the ground. Worry can have the same effect on you. It can gradually eat away at your heart and mind until it destroys you!

When we worry, we pre-image our future. Unfortunately, we do so with a negative outlook. Worry is asking the question, "What if..." and then answering it negatively. *What if I use my new float tube... and it doesn't hold me up... or I snag it with a hook as I lose a flipper off my foot... and a wind comes up and I can't get back to shore... and on and on and on.* That's worry!

You don't worry... do you? Actually, it's okay if you do. We all worry at times. Unfortunately, some turn worrying into a life-style.

They *choose* to worry about practically every situation they're in. The key word is *choose*.

Basically worry is fear, and it's a result of the Fall. Worry is the silent, deadly killer of faith. It distorts one of God's invaluable gifts to us—our minds. But God, through His Word, provides a solution for us in Isaiah 41:10:

> "Do not fear, for I am with you; do not be dismayed, for I am your God. I will strengthen you and help you; I will uphold you with my righteous right hand." (The *New American Standard Bible* says, "Do not anxiously look about you.")

This Scripture gives you confidence that (1) you have nothing to fear. Why? Because, I, God, am with you. (2) You should not be dismayed. Why? Because I am your God and I will strengthen you, help you, and uphold you. *Strengthen* means "to be alert or fortified." When you are unsure of a decision and need direction, you will be alerted and fortified. The word *help* in biblical Greek means "to surround." You will be protected on all sides. God will hedge you in with His protection. The word *uphold* means "to sustain." That means He keeps you going when the going gets tough.

So, with all that God promises, why worry? What really helps is to memorize Isaiah 41:10 for those times when you need encouragement.

Here's another passage that can make a difference:

> Don't worry about anything; instead, pray about everything; tell God your needs, and don't forget to thank him for his answers. If you do this you will experience God's peace, which is far more wonderful than the human mind can understand. His peace will keep your thoughts and your hearts quiet and at rest as you trust in Christ Jesus. . . . Fix your thoughts on what is true

and good and right. Think about things that are pure and lovely, and dwell on the fine, good things in others. Think about all you can praise God for and be glad about. Keep putting into practice all you learned from me and saw me doing, and the God of peace will be with you. (Philippians 4:6–9 TLB)

This verse changes lives. It cripples worry. How can it help you?

Take a blank 3 x 5 index card, and on one side write the word *STOP* in large, bold letters. On the other side write the complete text of Philippians 4:6–9. Keep the card with you at all times. When you begin to worry, find a place to be alone; take the card out; hold the STOP side in front of you, and say, "Stop!" aloud twice with emphasis. Then turn the card over and emphatically read the Scripture passage aloud twice.

Taking the card out interrupts your thought pattern of worry. Saying the word *Stop!* further breaks your automatic habit pattern of worry. Then reading the word aloud becomes the positive substitute for worry. (If you're in a group of people and begin to worry, follow the same procedure, only do it *silently!*)

Freedom from worry *is* possible! It requires that you *practice* the application of God's Word in your life. This means repetitive behavior. If you fail, don't give up. You may have practiced worrying for many years. Now you need to practice the application of Scripture throughout a longer period of time to completely establish a new worry-free pattern. It's possible.

So you also must be ready, because the Son of Man will come at an hour when you do not expect him.

—Matthew 24:44

Preparation and Presentation—
"The Right Cast"

46

*Jim Grassi tells the following story in his book *Promising Waters:**

> One of my favorite fishing stories comes from my good friend
> Jimmy Houston. Jimmy is one of the greatest anglers of all time.
> His winsome ways and jovial spirit have endeared him to the
> hearts of fishermen everywhere.
>
> Perhaps Jimmy's greatest asset is his love of the Lord with an
> unbridled passion. He continually applies God's Word to daily
> living. He is truly a disciple of the Lord Jesus.
>
> No one works harder at preparing for a tournament and pre-
> senting a lure correctly than Jimmy. He is a 14-time Bass Classic
> qualifier and has won every major casting contest he has entered.
> His underhand casting technique enables him to present rapid

casts to difficult areas with very little effort.

We have fished in the same boat many times. Jimmy usually operates in tight quarters in the midst of brush and trees. His presentations are extremely accurate and cover every predictable spot.

Needless to say, it is intimidating to compete against this champ. He is like a human vacuum cleaner, sucking up every fish within reach.

Years ago Jimmy was at a Bassmaster tournament and drew a local "good ol' boy" named Elton Jones as his partner. It was a bright calm day as the sun came up behind the docks. Elton, dressed in his bib overalls and plaid shirt, was standing at the appointed place with a big smile, a very large picnic basket, a single rod, and a little brown bag of fishing tackle.

Jimmy came by the dock and said, "Hop in, Elton. Where is your tackle?"

Elton replied, "I've got all I need, Jimmy. I'll be just fine."

As Jimmy took off from the docks, he couldn't help but think, "I surely won't have to worry about competition from Elton. This is going to be a snap."

Jimmy asked Elton if he wanted the first part of the day or the last half. It is customary for tournament fishermen to choose which part of the day they will take the front of the boat. The person up front gets to determine what part of the lake they want to fish.

Elton replied that he only wanted the front of the boat for one hour—from one to two o'clock.

After racing to the first spot, Jimmy began to make his rapid casts, frantically thrashing the water with his spinner bait. About 20 minutes passed when Jimmy realized Elton had yet to make a cast. Jimmy turned around to make sure Elton was still in the boat and discovered him sitting on the pro-throne seat with a large cup of coffee, eating a chocolate donut.

Elton smiled at Jimmy and said, "Want a cup of coffee or a donut?"

Jimmy politely refused, turned around, and just kept fishing, knowing that every cast was a new opportunity to introduce a fish to his spinner bait.

After an hour or so, Jimmy felt guilty that he had the water to himself and thought he ought to tell Elton it was okay for him to fish when he was on Jimmy's spot.

Elton said, "I am enjoying watching you work so hard, Jimmy."

After another hour, Jimmy hooked a fish and yelled to Elton to "get the net." Elton quickly obliged. He jumped off his chair and grabbed the net, scooping in a keeper fish. About a half hour later, Jimmy caught another one. Again, Elton scooped in the fish.

Elton still had not made a cast, or even set up his rod. Jimmy was beginning to wonder if Elton was one of Roland Martin's spies, taking notes on all Jimmy was doing. (Roland Martin, a winner of many bass tournaments, hosts a national TV show on fishing.)

Not much later Jimmy heard Elton moving around in the back of the boat. When Jimmy looked at Elton this time, he could not believe his eyes. Elton had taken the back seat off the deck and laid it on the floor between the two fishermen. He was spreading a large red and white checked tablecloth on the deck and was proceeding to unpack his picnic basket. He laid out a three-course, fried chicken lunch.

Elton asked, "Jimmy, how about taking a break and having some lunch?"

Jimmy thought, "I can't believe this guy. Doesn't he know that this is a major tournament and that every second counts?"

At one o'clock Elton picked up his lunch and began to rig his rod. Jimmy noticed a handful of mini-jigs (small lures) and some leader materials (high quality fishing line) that Elton was assembling. Jimmy looked at Elton and said, "Well, it's your turn. Where do you want to go?"

Elton said, "I would like you to pull away from this shoreline you've been beatin' on all morning and go out to the middle of the lake, about 300 yards from the little island." Jimmy reluctantly followed his orders and motored over to this quiet, nondescript area.

Looking around with some consternation, Jimmy asked, "Are you sure you want to be out here?"

Elton indicated it was the right spot, and said, "Keep an eye out for bait fish."

Elton stood up, grabbed his rod, and began to survey the water like a hawk looking for prey. Jimmy sat there with his spinner bait dangling, wondering how he was going to fish this open water.

Just about that time a large school of shad started dancing on the surface in an area about three times the size of the boat. Before Jimmy could evaluate the situation, Elton's cast was on the way with mini-jigs flying left and right.

As the jigs began to sink, Elton reached back and set the hook, yelling out, "One!" A few seconds later, he set the hook again, yelling out, "Two!" The routine was repeated until Jimmy heard, "Five!"

With his rod bent double, Elton shouted to Jimmy, "Son, get the net." With a proud look and his rod flexed to the maximum, old Elton slowly reeled in his limit of keeper fish while Jimmy tried to scoop them up.

Five fish were brought aboard just as the bait fish scattered and submerged for another day. Jimmy grabbed his rod, changed lures, and frantically peppered the water with casts as Elton was unhooking his trophies. Elton reminded him that it was all in the preparation and the presentation. For Jimmy, there were many valuable lessons learned that day about having the *right lure*, at the *right time*, in the *right place*.

It is not only thoughtful fishermen who realize the importance of preparation and presentation. Thoughtful disciples realize this as well.

As believers, we have a responsibility to prepare ourselves for the ministry. We are instructed, "Therefore, prepare your minds for action; be self-controlled; set your hope fully on the grace to be given you when Jesus Christ is revealed" (1 Peter 1:13).[40]

$\mathcal{L}$ife is unpredictable and unfair. It isn't always the way we want it to be. But how we respond to life is our choice.

So, Who's the Victim Here?

47

$\mathcal{B}$ass fishing is exciting. Just the anticipation of getting out on the water and searching for that spot is exciting. Even watching the sonar can be exciting.

We've come a long way with all the electronic gadgets we have to help us these days. I still have my first fish locator—a Lowrance Fish Lo-k-tor. A flashing light would indicate the bottom and then light up again when you found a fish. Today, everything is so sophisticated. Plus, we've got GPS to help.

In spite of all this, you could end up being rejected by Mr. Bass. I like what Shaw Grigsby said in his book: "It helps to remember that no matter how knowledgeable you are you can have a day when nothing works. Absolutely nothing. When you decided to go after bass, you picked a sport that has the potential to humiliate you."[41]

It's even worse when others are catching bass but you're not. I know. I've been there. It's these times when you've got to remember that there's a lot about bass fishing you just can't control. For example, think of all the variables you have to consider when you flip that bait on the water. When will he strike? Where will he hit it? Close to the boat or way out? How will he hit it—inhale it or barely be hooked? What's he going to do next? Jump? Run? Head for you? Go deep? Head for a log? Wrap it around a stump? And when he sees the boat? What then?[42]

With all this to think about, it's no wonder some anglers get overwhelmed. They approach bass fishing like they're the victim, making statements like:

"Oh man, I can't learn this lake. It beats me every time."

"Wow, this is *such* a problem. I don't know. . . ."

"I'll never get the hang of this stupid bait casting reel. . . ."

"Why does it have to happen like this? Every time I plan it always . . ."

And then there's the classic "if only—"

"If only the weather were better."

"If only those guys hadn't fished that spot so hard."

"If only the wind hadn't come up."

You know what we call these phrases? Victim phrases. This is victim thinking. It defeats you, cripples you, immobilizes you. And you know what? It's not because of what is happening around you. It's all in your head. It's your thoughts that do it. The Bible tells us, "As a man thinks in his heart, so is he" (Proverbs 23:7 THE MESSAGE). Unfortunately, some people live their lives based on negative thought patterns.

We hear a lot today about people being victimized by someone else. However, more people are victimized by their own beliefs and attitudes. By using these victim phrases we reinforce the control that problems have over our lives. Every time we think or say one of these phrases, we subconsciously begin to believe it and fulfill it. Eventually we talk ourselves into believing victim phrases are the truth. Look at them again.

"I can't." These words reflect three attitudes that keep us from moving on with our lives—unbelief, fear, and the lack of hope. When you say, "I can't," you're saying that you have no control over your life. But it's no harder to say, "It's worth a try." The results of this positive statement can be much more productive.

"That's a problem." Those who see life's complications as problems end up immersed in fear and hopelessness. It's true, life is full of barriers and detours. But with every obstacle comes an opportunity to learn, that is, if you have the right attitude. Using statements such as "That's a challenge," or "That's an opportunity for learning something new," leaves the door open for moving ahead.

"I'll never . . ." Stagnation. That's what this phrase reflects. It signals unconditional surrender to what is going on in your life. It doesn't give you or God an opportunity to work through whatever is happening. It's better to say, "I've never considered that before," or "I haven't tried it, but I'm willing to." This opens the door to change.

"That's awful." Sometimes this phrase is appropriate in view of a bad situation or bad experience we hear about. But in time we can learn to respond by saying, "All right, let's see what we can do about this," or "I wonder how I can help at this time," or "I wonder how I can do this differently."

"If only . . ." This phrase makes us into people imprisoned in lost dreams. A better, more positive phrase is "Next time . . ." which shows we haven't given up. We've learned from the past and we're getting on with our lives without regret.

"Why is life this way?" This is a normal response to the sudden

shocks of life. I've seen some people experience one hurt and setback after another and continue to ask this question over and over again for months, even years. They never make the transition to the "what" and "how" questions: What can I learn through this, and how can God be glorified through this?

"What will I do?" This question is initially a cry of despair. It's all right to ask. But in time we can learn to say, "I don't know what I can do at this moment, but I know I can handle this. Thank God, I don't have to face this issue by myself. I can learn and become a different person."

It's possible to limit our growth by what we believe and think. Some people live in a prison, locked in by negative thoughts and acting out their script.

Many years ago in a small town in the British Isles, a new jail was constructed that claimed to have an escape-proof cell. Harry Houdini, the great escape artist known all over the world, was invited to  come and test it to see if it really was escape-proof. He accepted the invitation, having once boasted that no jail could hold him.

Houdini entered the cell and the jailer closed the door behind him. Houdini listened to the sound of the key being slipped into the lock. The jailer withdrew the key and left. Houdini took out his tools and started to work on the cell door. But nothing seemed to work, and the hours passed. He was puzzled because he'd never failed to open a locked door.

Finally the great Houdini admitted defeat and leaned against the door. It suddenly opened. The jailer had never locked the door. The only place the door was locked—as you can guess—was in Houdini's mind.

I've done it. Perhaps you have, too. We've locked ourselves in be-cause of what we've thought. As a result we've stopped ourselves from being able to change. Having *joy* in your life is up to you—it's a choice. *Growth* in life is a choice. And *change* in life can be a choice. In most everything, choice comes before joy, growth, and change.

Tim Hansel, who survived a fall in a mountain-climbing accident and has been in pain for more than twenty years, writes,

> I've survived because I've discovered a new and different kind of joy that I never knew existed—a joy that can coexist with un-certainty and doubt, pain, confusion, and ambiguity. A journal entry a couple of years ago, written in the midst of the most try-ing period I've ever experienced, says simply, "I gave up looking for certainty—and found truth." I realized that when I quit wait-ing for certainty to come, I was free to discover, or rediscover, the essence of what I was really looking for.
>
> Joy is a process, a journey—often muffled, sometimes de-toured; a mystery in which we participate, not a product we can grasp. It grows and regenerates as we have the courage to let go and trust the process. Growth and joy are inhibited when we say "if only," enhanced when we realize that failures and difficulties are not only a critical part of the process, but are the very op-portunities to grow.[43]

You're probably familiar with the statement, "I'm ready to throw in the towel." John Karetji, a pastor from Indonesia, says that after he made that declaration during a difficult time in his life, a man came to him and asked if he knew the origins of the saying. The man said it came from boxing. When the manager standing outside the ring sees that his fighter can't make it any longer, he throws the towel into the ring, signifying that they are giving up.

Did you notice who has the towel? It's not the boxer. Only the one who sent the boxer into the ring can throw in the towel.

Although we may feel like the boxer who wants to call it quits, we were sent into the ring of life by someone else. Remember who sent you into the ring, for Jesus said, "I will never leave you nor forsake you," and "Lo, I am with you always."

These things I have spoken to you, that my joy may be in you, and that your joy may be full.

—John 15:11 RSV

Getting a Better View

48

ave you ever sunk a boat? I haven't, although I've tried. In fact, I tried pretty hard once, even though I didn't realize it.

I didn't know a whole lot about boats when I bought a 16-foot aluminum, all-around basic boat that had a Merc engine and a steering column. The first day I used it turned out to be an education.

After launching the boat in Lake Irvine, my friend parked the van and trailer while I stayed at the ramp holding on to a rope. When he returned we pulled the boat to the dock. As it came in we were amazed to see our lunches floating inside the boat.

"Did you put the plug in, Norm?"

"Ah . . . what plug?"

He just stared at me with a look of unbelief. Needless to say, we pulled the boat out, drained it, laughed a lot, inserted the plug, and got ready to leave. Some good ol' boys in the boat next to us watched the whole scene. Did they ever have a good time at our expense! They laughed and made wisecracks right and left. In fact, one of the guys said, "If I'd done something that dumb, it would ruin my whole day." We put up with the comments, then went out fishing.

When we returned, the other boat came in at the same time. And were the occupants ever in a foul mood! They hadn't caught a fish. One of the guys looked at us and asked, "Well, did you try to sink your boat again?"

"No, we figured out the plug. Besides, we were too busy catching fish."

"Huh? You caught some?"

"Sure we did—we each landed our limit." He didn't look too blessed when I said that. Oh well. We had a good day and I learned a lesson about boat plugs.

Perspective can make a big difference in life, whether fishing or doing anything else. For example, take the case of Fred, a landscape contractor. His first job was to remove a huge oak stump from a field. Fred had to use dynamite, but the only problem was he had never used it before. He was kind of nervous about it, especially with the old farmer watching his every move, so he tried to hide his jitters by carefully determining the size of the stump, the precise amount of dynamite, and where it should be placed for maximum effect. He didn't want to use too small an amount and have to do it over, nor did he want to use too much. He tried to go about it scientifically.

When Fred was ready to detonate the charge, he and the farmer went behind the pickup truck where a wire was running to the detonator. Fred looked at the farmer, said a silent prayer, and plunged the detonator. It worked . . . all too well. The stump broke loose from the ground, rose through the air in a curving arc, and plummeted right onto the truck's cab. Fred's heart sank. Not the farmer's. He was full of amazement and admiration. Slapping Fred on the back he said, "Not bad. With a little more practice you'll get it in the bed of the truck every time!"

Some of us are like Fred and some of us are like the farmer. We hit hard times and give in to discouragement, or we see how close we came to making it work and say, "Next time I'll get it right!"

Paul had something to say about our perspective in life: "But the fruit of the Spirit is love, joy, peace, patience, kindness, goodness, faithfulness, gentleness and self-control. Against such things there is no law" (Galatians 5:22–23). The fruit of the Spirit is joy. It's a realistic optimism, not the absence of hardship. It's choosing to smile when the tree stump lands on your truck or your boat begins to take on water through that little hole in the stern. It's saying, "It could be worse; I'll learn how to make it better." Which perspective do you live by?[44]

So when you're drained spiritually or emotionally, go to your power source—go to God.

Power Up

49

$\mathcal{B}$atteries vary in many ways—size, strength, and shape. Regardless of the kind you use for your boat or trolling motor, there's one battery you don't want to have—a dead one. Nothing can ruin a day's fishing like a dead battery. I know. I've had it happen.

Only trolling motors are allowed on one of the lakes I fish regularly. We're always hoping the battery will last as long as we need it. Our ears are tuned to the sound of a diminishing energy source. And yes, sometimes it happens. And then we keep hoping we can nurse enough out of it to get back to shore. But sometimes no matter how we turn the handle or reset the cable or yell at it, nothing happens. It's drained. It's dead.

Ever have mornings when you feel like that battery—drained and dead? The alarm goes off and you're supposed to roll out of bed. But you never make it. You don't have what it takes. You're like a depleted, disengaged dead battery.

Why do batteries die? Sometimes they've simply lived out their life expectancy. They've given all they were meant to, and now there's nothing left to recharge them. Others die because someone left a switch on, which drained the battery of its strength.

We're a lot like car batteries. We keep running and running without stopping to rest and recharge. All too soon we can't function. We've run out of strength. We call this *burnout*. The Scripture says, "Yet, I will rejoice in the Lord, I will be joyful in God my Savior. The Sovereign Lord is my strength; he makes my feet like the feet of a deer, he enables me to go on the heights" (Habakkuk 3:18–19).

If you and I want strength, we need to go to the power source, the Lord God. The statement "I will rejoice in the Lord" really means "to leap for joy and spin around in exultation." Not too many of us do this literally, but perhaps it wouldn't be a bad idea.

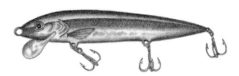

Do you know the difference between the words *joy* and *happiness* as they're used here? Happiness is based on having no problems or concerns. Joy means having faith in God, no matter what happens. When you trust in God rather than in your circumstances, you discover that God gives you the strength you need. And this strength will keep you moving ahead.

Therefore do not worry about tomorrow, for tomorrow will worry about itself. Each day has enough trouble of its own.

—Matthew 6:34

You're Casting a What?

50

$\mathcal{I}$'ve been known to do some "different" things. At least that's how I'd describe them. I'm sure some would use other words.

A recent discovery of mine was inspired by an article in one of the many bass fishing magazines I receive. And talk about different! This bass pro wrote about going to the East Coast for a tournament or show of some kind, but because of severe weather he was confined to his hotel room for two or three days. He was about to go stir crazy—not being able to get out there and connect with some bass—until he remembered something a friend had told him.

The friend suggested that when you can't engage in true bass fishing, try "flushin'." That's right, "flushin'." His friend said if you're in a hotel or home that has the newer jet-flush toilets, grab your rod, toss your bait in the bowl, flush it, and you'll get an unbelievable rush. (Now, as I read this, since I hadn't seen such a toilet, the only one that came to mind was the kind you find on aircraft like 757s. When you hit that lever it sounds like you're going to be sucked right down the drain. It's a giant roar.) Anyway, the bass pro thought he'd give it a try, so he flipped a 6-inch Sluggo into the hotel's jet-flush toilet and flushed it. It practically pulled the rod down the drain. He set the hook and that toilet ripped off 100 feet of line from his reel. He was standing there in his boxer shorts pulling on that doubled up bass rod and the drag was smokin' on the reel. He did it again and again, enjoying the rush from fightin' those sewer bass.

I shared this article with several friends and we had a good laugh over his antics. One evening my married daughter was visiting our house and read the article. Sheryl looked at me and asked, "Isn't that new toilet in your bathroom a jet?" I wasn't sure, but in unison we said, "Let's find out."

I went out to the garage, grabbed a rod and a Sluggo and headed to the bathroom. It's not very big, so I stood in the shower in order to drop the plastic into the toilet. Once there, I said, "Hit it!" and Sheryl flushed. The bait swirled in a circle for a while and then popped to the surface. We tried it a couple more times and realized, sadly, that our toilet was not of the jet variety. All this time my wife, Joyce, was standing outside the door. She wasn't saying much verbally, but those rolled eyes and the shaking of her head said volumes.

The next Sunday I was going to teach a class at my church on overcoming worry. I decided to share a Scripture passage written by the apostle Peter who, if you remember, was a fisherman. Peter was a man who struggled with faith, obedience, and fear in his life. Yet he learned to deal with his fear and wrote, "Cast all your anxiety on him because he cares for you" (1 Peter 5:7). It dawned on me how to illustrate this verse. Before leaving for church I went to the garage, grabbed the bass rod with the Sluggo tied on and tossed it in the car.

After I read and described the passage from first Peter to the large class of single adults, I took out the rod and said, "When the Scripture says, 'Cast your cares upon him,' this is what cast means." And with that I flipped the Sluggo through the middle of the audience. (There was no hook; I had just tied it on the line.) Several ducked, but it didn't hit anyone. I continued, "Now, many of you have perhaps already learned to cast or give or release your worries to the Lord. But there's a problem that many encounter. You'll notice that my bass rod also has a reel on it that holds the line. And on the reel is a handle that you turn when you want to retrieve the line. Some of you may be casting your worries on the Lord, but in no time at all you start reeling them back in and trying to deal with them yourself. What you need when you cast your anxieties away is a reel with no handle. Make it a one-way cast. No retrieving." They got the point. Several even commented on the illustration.

As we drove home from church Joyce echoed that it was a helpful illustration. But then she asked, "Ah, Norm, was that the rod you and Sheryl used the other night?"

I laughed and said, "Oh yeah, the same one."

"And was that the same bait you used in the toilet? You know, the one that swirled around and around, bouncing against the sides?"

"Oh yeah, the same Sluggo."

"Well, didn't you wash it off or anything like that?"

Oh-oh, I thought! "Ah . . . well . . . not really. . . ."

"Oh . . . well, just thought I'd ask." (Silence, then I was greeted by a familiar rolling of the eyes.)

It was still a good illustration, but next time, I might (not saying I will for sure, ya know) wash it off.

Lost and Found

51

$\mathcal{B}$ass fishing is enjoyable. But so is fishing for northern pike. The two fish have similarities. They're both voracious predators. They're not tentative coming after a lure. They slam it, almost ripping the rod out of your hand. In fact, I've had lures thrown back at me by both species.

Four of us were fishing for northerns at Betty Lake in Ontario, Canada. During the day a friend and my son-in-law were in a boat in the middle of the lake on a shallow weed bed. We heard a big commotion and cruised over to see what was happening. Both guys were leaning over the side looking for a pair of pliers they had dropped. They kept saying, "They've got to be here. It's not that deep. They've got to be here." The guys kept moving their boat around to where they thought the pliers had dropped, but after a while one set of reeds looked like another. Finally, they gave up and we all headed back to the cabin for some dinner before heading out again for more northern fishing.

That evening we passed near the weed bed. All of a sudden the other boat veered over to it. "One last look and we'll admit they're gone for good," we heard. Both guys were leaning over, looking into the clear water when my son-in-law just stood up and jumped in. When he came up, he had the pliers in hand. What are the odds of finding something like that in the middle of a lake? Valuable or not, it's great when something that's lost is found.

In 1997 we fished Alaska for both salmon and northerns. Here we tied into northerns over 20 pounds. And when four guys in a boat are hooked up at one time, it's bedlam. Still, it was great.

One morning the four of us were sitting in the boat anchored in the middle of the river while we fished for king salmon. My friend Gary had just cast out his red Storm Mag Wort lure so the current would catch it. All of a sudden we noticed an eagle swoop down from a tree and zero in on Gary's lure. It snagged the lure with its talons, then took off flying as fast as possible upriver. We heard the sound of its wings as it went by and someone said, "Gary, hang on to that rod or it's history, too!" We watched the eagle slowly disappear and heard the protest of the reel as the line was ripped off. It looked like Gary was going to be spooled. He was. Every foot of line was ripped off until, with a jolt, his rod and line parted.

We sat in stunned silence. After our initial shock wore off, we all started talking and laughing. We just hoped the hook hadn't snagged the eagle. About ten minutes later we noticed a red speck on the water upstream. As it floated toward us we realized it was Gary's lure! When the end of the line broke from Gary's reel, the jolt must have pulled the lure out of the eagle's grasp. Gary retrieved it to take home as a very unique trophy. Once again, we were delighted when something that was lost was found.

On yet another trip we were fishing in some small bays off of a river system. My partner and I noticed the guys in the other boat were going around and around in an ever smaller circle. We couldn't figure out why, so we went over. The explanation seemed far-fetched, but not really for these two. It seems they had caught a good-sized northern, but the line broke. Somehow the lure was wedged in its mouth in such a way that it couldn't dive, so it kept swimming around the surface in a circle. And these guys were chasing it as fast as they could. I kept hearing Ken say, "That's my best lure and I'm not going to lose it. We can do it. We'll catch this fish if it takes hours." Fish can out-smart people. And this one did its best for some time. But persever-ance paid off. Ken finally netted the northern, extracted his favorite lure, and released him unharmed. What a great experience to retrieve something that was lost.

Pliers can be lost and lures can be lost. But so can people. You've seen them. People who have no hope. That's how you were before Jesus became part of your life. So was I. Jesus said He came to seek and to save the lost. And how are those who are lost going to know about Jesus unless we share Him with them?

There was delight when the pliers were found, when the lure drifted back, and when the northern was netted. But this is nothing compared to the delight in heaven when a lost person is found. It happened when you were found. Perhaps there's someone you know who needs to know Jesus. There's nothing, absolutely nothing that compares to the experience of helping someone who is lost find a new life in Jesus.

And in the same way the Spirit also helps our weakness; for we do not know how to pray as we should, but the Spirit Himself intercedes for us with groanings too deep for words.

—*Romans 8:26 NASB*

Conversation Breakers

52

*H*ave you ever had difficulty talking with another person? You know, either they don't understand what you're saying or you have a hard time catching what they're talking about? Most of us have. Oh, there are reasons for these problems. Someone isn't listening or they seem to speak another language. I've been around guys on the lake who talk on and on and on. Pretty soon you tune out and hope they don't talk the fish to death. I've seen new anglers try to get advice from experienced guys who were either too busy, weren't listening, or didn't want to help. Sometimes you run into anglers with thick accents and you really feel dumb asking them to repeat the same phrase two or three times. You end up struggling just to talk.

Sometimes we struggle when talking to God. You'd think praying would be easy, but we make it into a big conversational problem. I've heard people voice frustrations like the following:

- The line was busy. (Translation: I don't think I got through to God.)
- God never answers. (Translation: I was too busy talking to hear His voice.)
- I didn't know what to say. (Translation: My mind wandered; I fell asleep; I really couldn't express my needs.)

Think about each excuse. They represent what AT&T calls the "busy signal." Busy, busy, busy! Sure, when you spend more time trying to get through to a person than actually talking to him or her, the experience can make you feel frustrated. Many feel this way about prayer. But God's Word tells us that He is never too busy to answer our calls. He always hears. He knows what we are going to say before we even say it. Scripture says, "Before they call, I will answer; while they are still speaking, I will hear" (Isaiah 65:24).

Another problem sometimes encountered on the phone besides a busy signal is receiving a call from a person who talks on and on and on. Picture the following scenario: A person asks a question, but he or she answers it before you even get your mouth open! You had something to say, but the person hangs up the phone before you have a chance to respond. You wonder why they called you in the first place. You've been violated by their unwillingness to hear you. Do you ever wonder if God feels that way when we call Him in prayer?

We cut short some of our conversations with God and often don't bother to wait for His answers after we pray. The chaplain of our U.S. Senate, Dr. Lloyd John Ogilvie, had something to say about this:

> God has more prepared for us than we are prepared to ask. We need to spend as much time seeking what God wants us to ask for as we do asking. Then our asking will be in keeping with His will. The desire to pray is God's gift. Prayer is not to get God's

attention, but to focus our attention on Him and what he has to say to us. Don't make prayer a one-way telephone conversation in which you hang up before you listen to what He has to say.[45]

Sometimes our struggles with prayer have more to do with our inability to focus than they do with our ability to talk and listen to God. Our minds begin to wander, and even when we are in the place of prayer, we are not really there. When sticking to prayer becomes a spiritual struggle, we need to call upon the Holy Spirit and ask Him to help us to pray.

I like to pray as I'm driving to the lake. I've also had some of the best times talking to God while I'm out in the boat fishing by myself, and I don't close my eyes either. I remind myself of several things: He always hears, He always cares, and I can tell Him anything. Then I close my mouth and listen to Him! Real conversations go both ways.

When you're struggling to pray, remind yourself of the power available to you. The Holy Spirit is more than able to pick up the slack if you will ask Him. That is His promise to you.

*How you see your problems will
determine whether they become
building blocks or stumbling blocks.*

Problem Solving

53

*Y*ou get out on the lake at the crack of dawn, pull into your favorite cove, lower the trolling motor, hit the switch and . . . nothing. You forgot to charge the battery. Another situation: You plan a trip for weeks only to have it wiped out by a windstorm. These things happen. We call them problems, and they're a normal part of life. They're all around us. Daily.

Problems can be related to the one you live with; where you live and how you live; where you work and with whom you work; how much money you have and what you believe about the money you don't have. They can be related to the trip you're planning, what happens on the trip, and the drive home.

James 1:2–3 says you *will* encounter problems: "Consider it pure joy, my brothers, whenever you face trials of many kinds, because you know that the testing of your faith develops perseverance." But you choose how you respond to problems. You can either view them as opportunities for growth or as excuses for failure. Another way to put it is a problem can end up being a profit or it can be a big loss.

There are five possible responses to any problem that enters your life. You could . . .

Curse the problem. Do this and you simply add a negative opinion to the negative facts of the situation. In other words, you compound the negativity. You've heard this coming from other boats if you've been fishing long!

Nurse the problem. You can choose to focus time and attention on the problem itself rather than on its solution. People like to talk more about problems than solutions. All this does is inflame the problem.

Rehearse the problem. Replay it until you're actually thinking about little else other than the problem.

Disperse the problem. This is a technique for tackling scientific problems. It requires breaking a problem down into its various parts, then working through each part until an answer is reached. As the smaller problems are solved, the big problem is also solved. This strategy is effective for all areas of our lives. Overwhelming problems can be solved when the smaller issues are dealt with one at a time.

Reverse the problem. Look for the positive. No situation or circumstance is 100 percent bad. There's got to be a glimmer of hope in every obstacle. Sometimes my wife, Joyce, thinks I'm a bit *too* positive. One day we were fishing a small lake and nothing was biting. We moved again and again from spot to spot. Around noon I announced, "Well, they're not biting here."

She said, "Oh, so we can go in now?"

"Go in? Why?"

"Well, we haven't even had one strike and we've tried several spots."

My response: "Well, at least we know where the fish aren't!"

So . . . what should you do when you encounter problems? Start by recognizing negativity for what it is—a distraction from a positive solution. Kick out the negativity. Of course, you can't ignore the problem, hoping that it'll go away. You dispose of the negative by: facing the problem and facing your negative response to it; making a conscious decision that a negative response is going to do nothing to solve the problem; and in that light, refusing to dwell upon the negative by turning instead to the positive. Only you can reverse the way you address a problem![46]

When it comes to solving a problem, look at what David did when he and his men were hiding from King Saul in caves (see 1 Samuel 19–24). David had a mess of problems. The men who accompanied him were described as being in distress, in debt, and discontented. As David stood before them, they were probably surprised when he declared, "I will bless the Lord at all times; His praise shall continually be in my mouth" (Psalm 34:1 AMP).

Praise at a time of despair. That's a shock! Have you ever done that? Praise when you're discontented? It may not come naturally, but it will turn your life around! Paul also learned the lesson:

> I know how to get along with humble means, and I also know how to live in prosperity; in any and every circumstance I have learned the secret of being filled and going hungry, both of having abundance and suffering need. I can do all things through Him who strengthens me. (Philippians 4:12–13 NASB)

*But seek first His kingdom and His
righteousness; and all these things
shall be added to you."*

—*Matthew* 6:33 NASB

Being the Best

54

$\mathcal{M}$ost of us want to learn. We want to become more proficient in our angling skills. At least I hope so. If you stay the same you stagnate.

Bass fishing features a lot of competition. At least it seems that way judging by all the tournaments. Some anglers admit they want to be the best—number one. Not only that, they say winning a title like Angler of the Year is an obsession. That word, *obsession*, best describes some anglers' pursuit—whether it's winning a national title or a local tournament or finally catching a double-digit bass. It's especially easy for men to become single-minded while pursuing a goal. Our brains are constructed that way.

Jimmy Houston, in his book *Caught Me a Big 'Un*, says winning Angler of the Year wasn't just a goal, it became his obsession. It's all he thought about on and off the water. Once he won the title, however, he went back to "his old lovable self," he says.

Winning tournaments has a lot of advantages. Win a B.A.S.S. tournament and your name gets out there. Win three and you're really known and noticed. Win the Classic and you're considered the best. Sponsors come to see you! Prestige and a great deal of money aren't just a dream anymore. They're yours! You're at the top. Your name is splashed all over magazines and newspapers. Your picture's taken again and again, perhaps with a Ranger boat, Quantam reels, or Shimano rods. The doors are opened to you. Who knows? You could end up feeling like a well-known man in the Old Testament who had it all: Solomon. He said, "I became greater by far than anyone in Jerusalem before me" (Ecclesiastes 2:9).

In today's society, reaching for the top is accepted. It's normal. We all want to move up the ladder. Each rung gets us closer to the top. But as we climb we need to ask ourselves several questions:

If you become the best in your field, *how will you feel when someone else takes your top place?* In the tournaments, whether amateur or pro, someone else will always step into your spot. And in your job there's always someone waiting in the wings. If you aren't producing, you'll be replaced!

What's the cost of striving to be best? When we become so set on a goal, we may miss out on enjoying the process of getting there. I overheard one angler telling another, "I've got a couple of sons that want to come fishing with me. But I can't concentrate with them here. I need to work on catching better fish if I'm going to get up that ladder. Someday, when they're older, I'll take them." After hearing that I wondered if "someday" would ever arrive. I'm glad I started my daughter fishing when she was four. And I even like it when she outfishes me!

Solomon went after prestige, power, and position, and he knew what it was like to reach the top. He couldn't go any higher. He was top dog. He was even greater than his own father. But it cost him—not just the nation, but also his son Rehoboam. Scripture says Rehoboam "did evil because he had not set his heart on seeking the Lord" (2 Chronicles 12:14). That's a high price to pay for being on top.

Finally, the most important question to ask is, *What rung of the ladder does God want you on?* He's got a claim on what we do with our life. We are called to live a life of excellence. That's great. But it doesn't mean we should always strive for the best position or the place of highest prestige.

Anyone who does not take his cross and follow me is not worthy of me.

—Matthew 10:38

Follow the Leader

The man's eyes were glued to the scope on the bow of his boat. His foot worked the controls of the trolling motor. He was getting a bit too close to where we were working a point. He glanced up, realized where he was, made a course correction, and with a grin said, "Sorry, I was so intent on following this school of fish, I wasn't paying attention."

Following is a common word in bass fishing. You could be following a flock of waterfowl that is following a school of baitfish, because you know bass could be following them. You could be following the contour of an underwater structure indicated by your fish locator. I've heard others say they're "following" the pro-tournament circuit during the year. And when I've been on the water and had trouble finding a spot I was told about, anglers have said, "Hey, I know where that is. Just follow me."

There's a lot of comfort in knowing where you're going. But have you ever thought about what or who you've been following throughout your life?

There is a story of two hunters who, while walking through the woods looking for deer, stumbled across an old farmyard. At first glance the two thought it was deserted. There were old car parts and tractor pieces lying about. The barn was in great disrepair, the fences needed mending, and the house was little more than a shack. The only evidence that it was still a working farm were the few chickens and a goat wandering about nearby. As they continued walking they came to a well near the middle of the property. Looking down the old well they noticed that they couldn't see the bottom and this started a conversation about just how deep that old well might be.

"I reckon there's only one way to find out how deep this well is," said one hunter. "We'll throw something down it, and then we'll listen for the splash."

"Good idea," replied the other, "What shall we send down the shaft?"

They looked around them, and the closest thing they saw was an old transmission lying on the ground nearby. Both men lifted the transmission over the edge of the well, dropped it, and listened. Although it was only a matter of seconds, it seemed like a long time to the men until they heard the "sploosh" of the transmission hitting the water below.

"That certainly is a *deep* one," commented one of the hunters.

"Sure is," replied the other.

As they turned to leave, the men were suddenly confronted with the goat they had seen earlier. The goat was charging right at them! Its head was down and it was running so fast that its feet barely touched the ground. At the last possible moment both men jumped aside and the goat charged right past them, bleating loudly, and fell straight down the well!

The men stared at each other, then at the well. Then at each other again. They had never seen anything like that before in their lives. They walked away from the well, shaking their heads in amazement at what they had just witnessed. They hadn't gone very far when they were approached by the farmer who owned the property. They chatted for a time, and the farmer gave them permission to hunt on his property. As they were about to leave the farmer asked, "By the way, have either of you fellows seen my goat?"

"Have we seen your *goat?!* Your fool goat tried to kill us. He charged at us and we barely had time to jump aside before he hit us. Luckily he missed—but he was going so fast that he ran right into the old well. That was a *crazy* old goat. You should have tied him up."

The farmer scratched his head and looked around him. "I thought I did have him tied up. In fact, I'm *sure* I had him tied up. I tied him to an old transmission."

The moral of the story is a simple, yet profound one: *You will follow what you're tied to!*[47]

Well, what are you tied to? Think about it, and remember who called us to follow Him. Several times Jesus said to others, "Follow me."

> Then Jesus said to His disciples, "If any one wishes to come after Me, let him deny himself, and take up his cross, and follow Me" (Matthew 16:24 NASB).

It's a good thing to be tied to Jesus.

Therefore, my beloved brethren, be steadfast, immovable, always abounding in the work of the Lord, knowing that in the Lord your labor is not in vain.

—1 Corinthians 15:58 RSV

The Waves of Life

$\mathcal{L}$et me tell you about a boat I owned. It was small. Quite small, in fact—12 feet. It was aluminum and stable but very generic. It only cost three hundred dollars, but it was all we needed for the 130-acre reservoir. At first we used oars but then graduated to a trolling motor. We even rigged a small umbrella for the hottest summer days. That boat saw a lot of bass come to its sides and then be released. It was also the same boat that was drenched by the fire-service helicopter.

My boat, along with fifteen to twenty others, was tied to a small dock one morning in the late fall of 1998 when a Santa Ana wind swept through Southern California. This is fairly common, and winds can get up to 50 miles per hour. But this one was much more intense. Some gusts hit 100 miles per hour as they swept over the reservoir. Needless to say, no one fished that day.

As the winds intensified, one of the workers at the impound went down to see how the dock was faring. It wasn't. It had split in two and numerous boats had broken loose. They were either beached or being blown away. As he stood there, an especially strong gust caused an empty fifty-gallon barrel to fly over his head and land in the lake.

A few days later I went out to fish but couldn't find my boat. I asked about it, but nobody had seen it. I looked all around but it was nowhere to be seen, so I borrowed another boat and set out fishing. As I approached the dam I noticed something in the water. I thought, *Could it be? Naw, it couldn't. But then again. . . .* When I got closer I recognized the bow of our boat sticking about a foot out of the water. It was stuck on rocks at the edge of the dam and looked pretty well beat up. I told the management about it and they said they'd get it out for us. Well, it took them a week to do so and during that time there was more wind, so the boat was in constant contact with those rocks. The day they pulled the boat out I called to see what shape it was in. "Norm, your boat's trashed. There are at least twenty dents and twenty holes in it. It looks like someone dropped it from an airplane. You won't believe it." When I saw it, I didn't believe it. It didn't really look like a boat anymore. It was bent out of shape, and in addition to the dents and holes, the aluminum on the bow had been peeled back in layers. The destructive power and force of those waves was awesome. The boat was history.

Waves have a way of disrupting our lives. They can throw us off course and disrupt our plans. You've got to watch out for them. Remember what happened with Peter and the waves?

> Immediately after this, Jesus told his disciples to get into their boat and cross to the other side of the lake while he stayed to get the people started home. Then afterwards he went up into the hills to pray. Night fell, and out on the lake the disciples were in trouble. For the wind had risen and they were fighting heavy

seas. About four o'clock in the morning Jesus came to them, walking on the water! They screamed in terror, for they thought he was a ghost. But Jesus immediately spoke to them, reassuring them. "Don't be afraid!" he said. Then Peter called to him: "Sir, if it is really you, tell me to come over to you, walking on the water." "All right," the Lord said, "come along!" So Peter went over the side of the boat and walked on the water toward Jesus. But when he looked around at the high waves, he was terrified and began to sink. "Save me, Lord!" he shouted. Instantly Jesus reached out his hand and rescued him. "O man of little faith," Jesus said. "Why did you doubt me?" And when they had climbed back into the boat, the wind stopped. The others sat there, awestruck. "You really are the Son of God!" they exclaimed. (Matthew 14:22–33 TLB)

Do you have waves in your life tossing you around? Most of us do from time to time. Peter was doing all right while he kept his eyes on Jesus. When he stopped looking at Him and stared at the waves he got into difficulty. It can happen to us. We have a choice of looking at the waves. This can terrify us. Or we can focus on Jesus. This can stabilize us. It's a choice we all have to make.

Be kind and compassionate to one another, forgiving each other, just as in Christ God forgave you.

—Ephesians 4:32

How Many Times?

57

$\mathcal{H}$ave you ever lain awake at night thinking about some of the profound questions of life such as:

If a turtle loses its shell, is it naked or homeless?

Why do we say something is out of whack? What's a whack?

Why is the person who invests all your money called a broker?

Do bass hold grudges?

Now *there's* one we can sink our teeth into. Just think about the life of a bass. It begins life having hundreds of brothers and sisters. But in no time at all, many of them end up as a meal for larger fish or birds. The bass has to be on alert as it grows. Now, if it's a female she has an advantage. In some areas females grow faster and live longer than males. As our bass gets larger she begins to notice some unique types of food (or so she thinks) being presented to her. You know, wooden or plastic plugs, metal blades on a thin bent wire, and all sorts of plastics. It's a great diet. And all these offerings come with a special benefit—a sharp hook. In fact, some even have treble hooks. If her area is fished heavily she could be caught numerous times. And on occasion she could get a ride on a line to a spot where she's weighed and photographed, perhaps earning lots of money for the angler who reached down and lifted her out of the water by the bottom lip.

Do you wonder if any bass remember? And just suppose they carry a grudge. And then, what might happen if they grew, oh say, to 100 or 150 pounds? I remember a movie titled *Revenge of the Nerds*. This one might be called *Revenge of the Bass*. I'd hate to meet a mad, predatory, aggressive bass who remembered I'd caught him on several occasions. Fortunately, we can all breathe easy. Bass don't carry grudges. They're not resentful. Not like some people I know.

In a way, bass are the fortunate ones. They don't really remember offenses. We do, especially if the person does something to us again and again and again. We store up the slight or hurt and begin dwelling on it. It grows to resentment. And then we think it's payback time. That's one way to live life. I guess it's the world's way. There's another choice, though. Jesus talked about it:

> Then Peter came and said to Him, "Lord, how often shall my brother sin against me and I forgive him? Up to seven times?" Jesus said to him, "I do not say to you, up to seven times, but up to seventy times seven" (Matthew 18:21–22 NASB).

C. S. Lewis talked about it in *Letters to Malcolm*: "To forgive for the moment is not difficult. But to go on forgiving, to forgive the same offense again every time it recurs to the memory—there's the real tussle."

And Ken Gire offered a prayer about it. Perhaps his thoughts can help you when forgiveness is needed:

Lord,
How often do I forgive?
I'm asking not for an answer, only for an opportunity to come clean.
How often do I forgive?
"Search me, O God, and know my heart."
How often do I forgive the gossiper in my life?
How often do I forgive the exaggerator? The out-and-out liar?
How often do I forgive the talker in my life? The interrupter?
The person who sits around like a bump on a log and says nothing?
How often do I forgive a boss who's demeaning?
A coworker who's competing for my job?
How often do I forgive my mother, for all she did or didn't do?
My father for all he said or didn't say? My brother? My sister?
"Try me and know my anxious thoughts."
How long is my mental list of hurt feelings?
How far back does the account of "wrongs suffered" go?
"And see if there be any hurtful way in me."
How many people do I mumble to myself about, mentally rehearsing the scene where I tell them off and expose them to the world?
How many times do I hear bad news about someone who's hurt me, and I'm glad because, after all, they had it coming?
"And lead me in the everlasting way."
Forgive me, O God, for all the times I haven't forgiven. For all the times I've only partway forgiven, or grudgingly forgiven, or self-righteously forgiven. Lead me into a better way of living, which can only be found in a better way of forgiving. Help me

to forgive others the way you have forgiven me.
  Not for a moment but for a lifetime.
  Not seven times . . . *every* time.[48]

℃rust in the Lord with all your heart and lean not on your own understanding; in all your ways acknowledge him, and he will make your paths straight.

—Proverbs 3:5–6

"I Lost Him"

58

"I lost him." A common phrase in fishing. Most of the time it's used when a bass strikes and we miss connecting with him or he jumps and throws the line. Other losses can happen, too. You've probably experienced some of these. For example, you pick up your favorite lure to tie it on and you drop it . . . overboard. And it's not a floater, either.

My fishing partner was out fishing by himself with an outfit I had sold him a month earlier, a Corsair reel and a Lamiglas rod. It wasn't cheap. He tossed out a spider jig, set the rod down to straighten out something else in the boat, and a fish struck—sending the rod and reel over the back of the boat. Needless to say, my partner wasn't a happy camper. To top it off, this was the second time the lake had eaten one of his outfits.

Three months later we were fishing in the same area. It had been a good morning. We'd caught and released a dozen largemouth. We were letting a gentle wind propel us along and casting to spots when he hooked on to something. "This is weird," he said. "It sure doesn't feel like a fish, but there's something on there." I thought it was probably a branch or some snag, so since I was closer to his line I began to bring it in by hand for him. All of a sudden I was pulling up the tip of a rod followed by the whole outfit. As soon as we saw it, our eyes got big and we started to yell and laugh. Yup, you guessed it—his lost rod. Anglers in other boats could hear us and yelled encouragement back. For the rest of the day, about every fifteen minutes one of us would look at the other, shake our head and say, "I don't believe it." I don't know how many people later told him, "With your luck you ought to go to Vegas or buy a lottery ticket." Months later they were still talking about the guy who hooked his lost rod. It *was* a great day.

Have you ever felt lost? Many of us have. I've seen hikers lost in the mountains and anglers lost on a river system. It's not a happy feeling. It's that sense of being out of control. Once that happens a sense of dread or even panic begins to grow. Unfortunately, this doesn't help in trying to think through the problem. Fortunately, most find their way back.

There are other ways of being lost in life. It's more of a sense or a feeling. As a counselor, I often hear the phrase, "I feel so lost right now." We can know where we are physically, but we may feel lost when it comes to a direction for our lives. Or we can feel lost emotionally. It's difficult to sort out what we're feeling. We can also be lost spiritually—even as a Christian. When you're lost like this, you feel like you've been cut adrift and you're at the mercy of the elements. I've been there.

Several years ago eight of us decided to float the Snake River from Jackson Lake dam to a well-known entrance to the park, Moose Junction, a distance of about twenty-five miles. We had floated portions of the river with guides several times so we decided it would be fun to try it on our own this time. We went to the forest service and asked for a map showing all the obstructions on the river.

The morning of the trip we went to the river and blew up the two four-man rubber rafts. To test our work we had one of the couples sit on one of the rafts to see if it needed more air. Well . . . the man weighed 300 pounds, and when they both sat in the raft it sort of folded up around them, engulfing them. It reminded me of a scene out of *Jaws*. It was pretty obvious we needed more air in the rafts.

Finally we launched. We paddled and after a while hit a very slow stretch of water. Here we made a fateful decision (some have suggested other words for it). To have more fellowship we decided to tie the two rafts together with a rope. It seemed like a good idea at the time. We failed to realize this cut down our ability to steer the rafts. So we were even more susceptible to the currents and often had to drift along with them.

For several hours everything went well. A large tourist raft with about twenty-five people on it was about 100 yards ahead of us. All of a sudden we rounded a big S-curve where another river joined the Snake. There was a tremendous surge of water where the two rivers met. We hit that spot and our rafts took off downstream, totally out of control. With no steering, we went where the current took us. All of a sudden we noticed a log jam dead ahead. It *wasn't* on the forest service map. One raft was being pulled to the left of the jam, the other to the right. So we nailed that jam dead center. We were stuck with water sloshing in. I pulled out a knife and cut the rope so the one raft could float off. It did. About a hundred feet downstream it sunk in four feet of water and the four occupants walked to shore. But our raft was still stuck at the log jam. We had ballast. Yes, the 300-pound rafter was helping to hold the raft to the log jam!

Now, have you ever done something kind of dumb or awkward like miss the last step at the bottom of a stairs and stomp down hard? You look around to make sure no one saw you, right? Well, it would have been great if we could have crashed in private. No such luck. Remember the tourist raft? It seems that the guides of that raft had sensed what would happen to us so they pulled to shore before we ever arrived. Here they were—twenty-five people all lined up with their still and video cameras capturing our fiasco and laughing. Since the water wasn't that deep the guides waded out and helped us get unstuck. They were nice enough to take us in their raft to our destination.

Nine hours in a raft made for a long, eventful day. Later that night we talked for two hours over a great dinner in the lodge, sharing our feelings of being out of control as we hurtled toward the log jam. We all wished we could have steered our rafts instead of just drifting so much with the currents.

If you're looking for direction in any area of your life, if you feel lost emotionally or spiritually, don't just consult with yourself. When I want to learn how to fish a new lake, I find someone who's been there many times or hire a guide. You and I have a guide for our life. Go to His Word.

God is leading you as He's led others. Remember a man named Abraham? God led him from the security of his home to an unknown land. What did Abraham do? "By faith Abraham obeyed when he was called to go out to the place which he would afterward receive as an inheritance. And he went out, not knowing where he was going" (Hebrews 11:8 NKJV). When you're willing to follow God, you will eventually find the security and landmark you're looking for in your life. You may not know the timing or where you'll end up, but that's all right. He does.

We are successful when we obey God's Word—when we are faithful to what He calls us to do.

Finding Success

59

Success. It drives us, stymies us, frustrates us, eludes us, dominates us. Let's admit it. We all want to be successful at something (especially catching fish). We are taught to be successful. We're told we need to be successful. We live in a success-dominated society. We're urged to "go for it."

Vince Lombardi, one of the best-known football coaches of all time, said, "Winning isn't everything—it's the *only* thing!" He applied that to football. Others apply it to life. We're always trying to succeed at something. But like anything else, striving for success puts us out of balance. Success can become addictive. It can even destroy us.

Our view of success reflects our values. All of us—parents, students, ministers, gang members, police officers, burglars—are driven by what we value. Our values are reflected in the way we use our time and energy.

A fisherman lying on the bank of a river in Maine was having a great time. He would cast his line into the gently moving water, and now and then he caught a silver salmon. He had his lunch and beverage by his side as he sat in the shade of a tree. His stringer was getting heavy with the weight of the fish.

He was bringing in another large fish when a well-dressed businessman drove up and came over to him. "Don't you know that you could catch many more fish if you would put several lines in the water?" he asked.

The fisherman replied, "Why would I want more fish?"

"Well, look, it's simple," the businessman said. "If you had more lines, you'd catch more fish and make more money. You could buy a fishing boat. Once you did that, you could open up a store and sell your fish to everyone. After you open one store, you could open several others. You'd employ people, and eventually you could become a fish wholesaler and ship fish all over the country. And then you would become very wealthy."

The fisherman took a bite of his sandwich but looked skeptically at the businessman. "And then what would I do?" he asked.

"Well, if you've become that successful, you'd have all the time you want to do what you enjoy the most. You could lie back, relax, and go fishing."

The fisherman smiled and said, "But that's what I'm doing now."

This fisherman's values were reflected in how he used his time. He knew he was successful, even though it was not apparent to other people. He knew that his success was not measured by how much he owned or how much money he had but by his sense of inner contentment. The fisherman knew that success is something internal rather than external.[49]

Are you like the fisherman? Will you know success when you see it, or will you keep pursuing an illusion? Terry Hershey says, "We live in a weird world where more is never enough." We cannot be content, so we fantasize about those who have "arrived" by reading about lifestyles of rich and famous people; we sacrifice the values of our ordinary life of relationships, family, and personal solitude to pursue the ecstasy of that which will let us "be somebody." The fisherman knew he was somebody. He had found his ecstasy in a simple pleasure.

What is the biblical measure of success? When God was preparing Joshua to lead the Israelites into the Promised Land, he laid out for Joshua the criteria for success: "Be careful to obey all the law my servant Moses gave you; do not turn from it to the right or to the left, that you may be successful wherever you go. Do not let this Book of the Law depart from your mouth; meditate on it day and night, so that you may be careful to do everything written in it. Then you will be prosperous and sucessful" (Joshua 1:7–8).

Success comes from being faithful to God and His ways. Is this how the world defines success? Usually not. But it will lead to contentment and a sense of satisfaction that we have done the right thing.

In his book *Guard Your Heart*, Gary Rosberg describes success in an appealing way:

> Success is not just a matter of money, power, and ego, but also issues of the heart—like compassion, kindness, bravery, generosity, love.
>
> It's an issue of character, not performance.
>
> It's an issue of being the person God designed you to be, not how much salary you can pull down in a year.
>
> It's an issue of who you really are, not how many notches you

can rack up on your resume or the shape of your car's hood ornament.

There's a shift now in our culture. Success hasn't cut it. But significance has more meaning.

Who makes us significant? I believe it is a Person. Not your boss, kids, parents, or even you. What makes you and me significant is the Person of Jesus Christ. He created us in order to glorify Himself. That's our job in life, to bring honor and glory to Him. He is the one who makes us significant.[50]

If God chose to write you a letter about success and His expectations of you, what might He say? In his book *The Seven Seasons of a Man's Life*, Patrick Morley suggests that such a letter might look like this:

Dear Son,

I am writing because I want you to stop and take stock of your life. I want you to look closely at the way you have lived your life. I want you to make changes based on a new commitment to My larger purposes for your life and the world—while you still have time.

I am going to give you some things to ponder. Do this in a quiet place either early in the morning or late at night, when it is still and quiet. Don't be in a rush. Give yourself plenty of time. Think it over.

You have wanted success. Success is elusive, isn't it? That's because you have been living by your own ideas. I do want you to be successful, but on My terms, not yours. You measure success in the quantity of your possessions and achievements. I measure success in the quality of your character and conduct. You are interested in the success of your goal. I am interested in the success of your soul. True success is to satisfy your calling, not your ambition. Live as a called man.

He is successful who is found faithful to do the will of God. Are you seeking to know and do My will? Or are you succeeding in a way that doesn't really matter to Me? Would you be willing to live the rest of your life in obscurity if that is My will?

I made you with dignity. I created you to be significant. I have put in you the spark of divinity. You are My crowning achievement. You are the full expression of My creative genius. You are My most excellent creation. I was at My very best when I created you. Do you understand and believe what I have just said?

Be careful not to overemphasize either your significance or your insignificance. If you think too highly of yourself, you will lose your humility and brokenness before Me and think there is nothing you cannot do.

The biggest problem I see in your life is that you have spent your whole life looking for something worth living for. It would be better if you found something worth dying for. Give your life to that, and I will give you joy, no matter how hard the path becomes. What is the cause you would be willing to die for? Better still, who is the one you would be willing to die for? How, then, should you reorder your life?

I want you to reflect carefully on what I am about to say. Success that really matters depends on a few key areas: having a close moment-by-moment walk with Me, finding fulfilling work, modeling a life of integrity, living within your means, maintaining your health (My temple), establishing loving relationships, living a life of good deeds, and coming to live with Me when you die.

What changes should you make in the brief time you have remaining? How would you live if I told you that you have only one year left on earth? One month? One week? One day?

Live your life in the shadow of the cross. Soon, you will see Me face-to-face.

Eternally yours,

Your heavenly Father[51]

*Lead me in thy truth, and teach
me, for thou art the God of my
salvation; for thee I wait
all the day long.*

—*Psalm 25:5* RSV

A Prayer for Today and Every Day

60

$\mathcal{Y}$ou know what it's like to head for the dock at the end of a day of fishing. It's over, but it's not. There's another day ahead.

You've come to the end of a journey in this book, as well. But since it was about living a life of faith in Jesus, it's not over. It continues on forever. It never ends. Whether we experience a day on the lake, in our home, or on the job, we're there to make a difference. Our lives can be different because of knowing Jesus. And we can help others be different, too, by introducing them to Jesus.

I'd like to conclude this book with a simple prayer. Perhaps you could read it aloud and ask your Heavenly Father to guide your life.

O God, my Father, I want to thank you that you sent your
Son Jesus Christ into this world to be my Savior and Lord.
I thank you that He took our body and our flesh and blood

upon himself, and so showed me that this body of mine is fit to be your dwelling place.

I thank you that He did my work, that He earned a living, that He served the public, and so showed me that even the smallest tasks are not beneath your majesty and can be done for you. Help me to realize that serving you and others is what I've been called to do.

I thank you that He lived in an ordinary home, that He knew the problems of living together, that He experienced the rough and smooth of family life, and so showed me that any home, however humble, can be a place where in the ordinary routine of daily life all of life can be made an act of worship to you.

Lord Jesus, come again to me this day.

Come into my heart and cleanse it, that I then being pure in heart may see God our Father.

Come into my mind and enlighten it, that I may know you, who are the Way, the Truth, and the Life.

Touch my lips, so I don't speak any word that would hurt another or offend you.

Touch my eyes, that they may never linger on anything that I shouldn't be looking at.

Touch my hands, that they may become useful with service to the needs of others. Help me to treat others with patience, kindness, and compassion.

When I am sad, comfort me; when I'm tired, strengthen me; when I'm lonely, cheer me up; when I'm tempted, help me to resist; when I'm happy, help me to remember that you are the source of this happiness.

O God, our Father, help me to live in such a way that whenever your call comes for me, at morning, at noon, or at evening, it may find me ready, my work completed, and my heart at peace with you, so that I may enter into your presence and into life eternal; through Jesus Christ our Lord. Amen.[52]

Notes

1. *Largemouth Bass—An In-Fisherman Handbook of Strategies*, (Brainerd, Minn., 1980), 1–31, adapted; Shaw E. Grigsby, Jr. with Robert Coram, *Bass Master Shaw Grigsby—Notes on Fishing and Life* (Washington, D.C.: National Geographic Books, 1998) 15, adapted.
2. Jimmy Houston, *Caught Me a Big 'Un . . .* (New York: Pocket Books, 1996), 99–100, adapted.
3. Gary Rosberg, *Guard Your Heart* (Sisters, Ore.: Multnomah, 1994), 15–17, adapted.
4. Original source unknown.
5. Patrick Morley, *The Seven Seasons of a Man's Life* (Nashville: Thomas Nelson, 1995), 205–206.
6. A. W. Tozer, *The Knowledge of the Holy* (New York: Harper Brothers, 1961), 61–62, adapted.
7. J. I. Packer, *Knowing God* (Downers Grove, Ill.: InterVarsity, 1973), 68–73, adapted.
8. Jim Grassi, *Heaven and Earth* (Eugene, Ore.: Harvest House Publishers, 1997), 23–25.
9. Tom Sullivan, adapted from a speech given to the Million Dollar Round Table Annual Meeting, 1983.
10. Sullivan.
11. Ken Gire, *Reflections on the Word* (Colorado Springs, Colo.: Chariot Victor, 1998), 40–41.
12. Charles R. Swindoll, *The Finishing Touch* (Dallas, Tex.: Word, 1994), 148.
13. Morley, 204.
14. Jim Grassi, *Promising Waters* (Eugene, Ore.: Harvest House, 1996), 23–26.
15. Clifford Nobarius and Howard Markman, *We Can Work It Out* (New York: G. P. Putnam Sons, 1993), 70–73, adapted.
16. *Largemouth Bass—An In-Fisherman Handbook of Strategies,* 68, adapted.

17. Houston, 108.
18. Joe E. Brown, *Battle Fatigue* (Nashville: Broadman & Holman, 1995), 14–15, adapted.
19. Tim Hansel, *When I Relax, I Feel Guilty* (Elgin, Ill.: David C. Cook, 1979), 55.
20. Charles R. Swindoll, *Strike the Original Match* (Sisters, Ore.: Multnomah Press, 1980), 92.
21. Grigsby with Coram, 39, adapted.
22. Judson Edwards, *Regaining Control of Your Life* (Minneapolis: Bethany House Publishers, 1989), 48, adapted.
23. Wallace Terry, "When His Sound Was Silenced," *Parade Magazine* (December 25, 1994): 12–13, adapted.
24. Gary Oliver, *How to Get It Right After You've Gotten It All Wrong* (Wheaton, Ill.: Victor, 1995), 20–25, adapted.
25. Jim Grassi, *In Pursuit of the Prize* (Eugene, Ore.: Harvest House Publishers, 1999), 126–27.
26. Dr. Sidney Simon, *Getting Unstuck* (New York: Warner Books, 1988), 14, adapted.
27. Brown, 51–52, adapted.
28. "Jay and Clay—Two Kindred Bassing Spirits," *Bassmaster* (May 1999): 92 SW–1–4, adapted.
29. Jim Goodwin, "The Impossible Is the Untried," in Mark Templeton's *Discovering the Laws of Life* (New York: Continuum, 1994), 31–32, adapted.
30. H. Norman Wright, *What Men Want* (Ventura, Calif.: Regal Books, 1996), 158–161, adapted.
31. Ken Gire, *The Reflective Life* (Colorado Springs, Colo.: Chariot Victor Publishers, 1998), 86.
32. Gire, *Reflections on the Word*, 122–123.
33. Tim Ritter, *Deep Down* (Wheaton, Ill.: Tyndale House Publishers, 1995), 141, adapted.
34. Adapted from a quote by Joseph Shore in Lloyd Cory, *Quotable Quotations* (Wheaton, Ill.: Victor Books, 1985), 55.
35. Tim Hansel, *Holy Sweat* (Dallas: Word, 1987), 54–55.
36. John C. Maxwell, *Be a People Person* (Chicago: Victor Books, 1996), 122–24, adapted.
37. Shawn Morey, *Incredible Fishing Stories* (New York: Workman Publishers, 1994), 5–6, adapted.

38. Morey, 11–12, adapted.
39. James C. Dobson, *Straight Talk to Men and Their Wives* (Waco, Tex.: Word Books, 1980), 136.
40. Grassi, *Promising Waters*, 39–43. Used by permission.
41. Grigsby with Coram, 104.
42. Ibid., 112, adapted.
43. Tim Hansel, *You Gotta Keep Dancin'* (Colorado Springs, CO: David C. Cook, 1985), 90–91.
44. Rites, 52, adapted (original source unknown).
45. Dr. Lloyd John Ogilvie, *God's Best for My Life* (Eugene, Ore.: Harvest House Publishers, 1981), 8.
46. William Mitchell, *Winning in the Land of Giants* (Nashville: Thomas Nelson, 1995), 27–28, adapted.
47. Dr. David Beighley, *Dancing With Yesterday's Shadows* (Muskegon, Mich.: Gospel Film Publications, 1997), 161–62.
48. Gire, *Reflections on the Word*, 100–101.
49. Carole Hyatt and Linda Gottlieb, *When Smart People Fail* (New York: Simon & Schuster, 1987), 206–08.
50. Gary Rosberg, *Guard Your Heart* (Sisters, Ore.: Multnomah, 1994), 138–39.
51. Morley, 151–156.
52. William Barclay, *A Barclay Prayer Book* (London: SCM Press, Ltd., 1963), 8–9, adapted.